the Cocktail Edit

**EVERYTHING YOU NEED TO
KNOW ABOUT HOW TO MAKE
ALL THE DRINKS THAT MATTER**

by Alice Lascelles

FOR ALL THOSE WHO TEND BAR AT THEIR KITCHEN TABLE

MANAGING DIRECTOR: Sarah Lavelle

SENIOR COMMISSIONING EDITOR: Céline Hughes

ART DIRECTION AND DESIGN: Maeve Bargman

DESIGN DIRECTION: Emily Lapworth

PHOTOGRAPHER: Laura Edwards

COPY EDITOR: Nick Funnell

ASSISTANT EDITOR: Sofie Shearman

PRODUCTION CONTROLLER: Nikolaus Ginelli

HEAD OF PRODUCTION: Stephen Lang

First published in 2022 by Quadrille,
an imprint of Hardie Grant Publishing
Quadrille
52–54 Southwark Street
London SE1 1UN
quadrille.com

Cataloguing in Publication Data: a catalogue record for this book is available from the British Library.

ISBN: 978 1 78713 864 3

Printed in China

CONTENTS

INTRODUCTION   4

INGREDIENTS   8

EQUIPMENT   40

TECHNIQUES   50

RECIPES   80

THE GIN SOUR 82

THE MARTINI 88

THE OLD FASHIONED 94

THE DAIQUIRI 100

THE NEGRONI 106

THE MANHATTAN 114

THE MARGARITA 120

THE SPRITZ 128

THE GIMLET 134

THE WHISKEY SOUR 140

THE HIGHBALL 146

PUNCHES & CUPS 152

A FEW MORE DRINKS
EVERYONE SHOULD
MAKE ONCE IN THEIR LIFE 160

INDEXES   170

INTRODUCTION

Before you read any further, go and put a couple of cocktail glasses in the freezer. Because you'll be needing them later.

Done that?

Good – then let's begin.

There are thousands, if not millions, of cocktails in the world, with all sorts of flavours and names. But most of them are really, in essence, just twists on a handful of classic drinks. A Mint Julep is just an Old Fashioned served over crushed ice and mint; a Boulevardier is a Negroni fortified with bourbon instead of gin; a French 75 is just a simple gin sour with a decadent slosh of champagne.

It was this realisation that really unlocked cocktails for me. It got my nose out of the recipe book – and Google – and allowed me to mix more intuitively. And the whole point of making cocktails, after all, is that you bring something of yourself to the drink – otherwise you might as well just open a bottle of wine or buy in ready-made cocktails..

The Cocktail Edit is built around the 12 classics I make the most; the Martini, the Negroni, the Manhattan and so on – drinks you'll almost certainly know. Each chapter encompasses one of these, as well as six variations on the theme; some of them are related classics, some are contemporary twists, a few are recipes by me.

You'll see how easy it is to reinvent a Daiquiri with watermelon, basil or Green Chartreuse, or to re-mix a Spritz with rosé wine or sparkling jasmine tea. You'll discover what a smoky malt can do for a Martini and how to make a showstopping Whiskey Sour with last night's red wine. You'll master all the classics that matter – and, I hope, get ideas for hundreds more drinks besides.

Over half the cocktails featured in this book can be made with just 12 bottles. But there are suggestions on what to do with those oddities at the back of the drinks cupboard, too. I've kept tools and glassware to a minimum. You won't need a *sous vide* or a Hoshizaki ice machine. This is a book designed for people who bartend at their kitchen table – people, in other words, like me.

The things that make a cocktail really great are often very simple details – the frozen glass, the lemon twist – that transform two fingers of alcohol into an ice-glazed elixir. Tricks of the trade are covered in Ingredients, Equipment and Techniques – before you dive into Recipes, please do give them a read.

And take time, as you prepare your cocktail, to savour everything you do – as I was reminded so many times while writing this book, the crack of ice, the clink of glasses, the smell of fresh mint and lime can be intoxicating too.

Those glasses you put in the freezer should be good and cold by now. Time to assemble your ingredients. It's almost cocktail hour…

HOW THIS BOOK WORKS

Getting the basics right is crucial when it comes to making cocktails – so the first half of *The Cocktail Edit* is dedicated to ingredients, tools and techniques. If you come across something later on in the book that you don't know how to make or do, you will probably find it here.

The second half of the book contains 100 cocktail recipes divided into 13 chapters. Each chapter begins with a classic cocktail, such as a Negroni or Gimlet, and then explores six variations on the theme. In most cases it's the ingredients or formula that these recipes have in common. But just occasionally – as in the case of Punches & Cups – it's more the occasion or mood. (The exception to all this, as you may notice, is chapter 13, which contains 16 drinks that have nothing in common except for the fact that I couldn't bear to leave them out.)

The indexes at the back have been designed so you can search by cocktail name or flavour. There is also an alternative index that groups recipes along more thematic lines: 'Trashy', 'Secret handshakes', 'Cooling cocktails for hot days'.

INGREDIENTS

DRINKS CABINET

You don't need expensive spirits to make good cocktails – what you need are spirits that are good team players. The sort of classic, well-made brands that, happily, often reside at the more affordable end of the spectrum.

If you just bought gin, sugar, lemons and limes, you certainly wouldn't go thirsty – you'll find lots of riffs on these four ingredients in the chapters on *The Gin Sour – p. 82* and *The Gimlet – p. 134*.

If you could stretch to gin, bourbon, red vermouth, dry vermouth, Campari and a bottle of cocktail bitters, you'd have a 6-bottle bar and the makings of a formidable drinks cabinet. One that could do the Martini, Negroni, Old Fashioned, Manhattan (and many twists thereon) and a whole host of other classics besides (**see** *The 6-Bottle Bar – p. 173*, for ideas).

You could not, of course, do either the Daiquiri or the Margarita. And I couldn't leave those out. So I've based *The Cocktail Edit* around the 12 bottles I use the most.

With a bit of judicious shopping, you could get all 12 bottles listed opposite for under £200. (Online retailers The Whisky Exchange and Master of Malt are two great places to look.) Armed with these, some fruit and mixers, you can make the majority of the drinks in this book. (**See** *The 12-Bottle Bar – p. 173*, for ideas).

I've also included a selection of spirits that are not essential, but nice to have (every bottle listed in this section is used in *The Cocktail Edit* more than once); plus a list of specialities that make only a fleeting appearance, just in case you've been wondering what on earth to do with that bottle of Bénédictine DOM.

Where possible, I've kept ingredients generic. But in the instances where only one brand will do – such as Luxardo Maraschino Liqueur – I've mentioned it by name. If you wish to search by a particular flavour, **see** *The Index – p.171*.

THE 12-BOTTLE BAR

GIN

DRY VERMOUTH

RED VERMOUTH

BOURBON OR RYE WHISKEY

CAMPARI

COGNAC

RUM

TEQUILA

TRIPLE SEC

COCKTAIL BITTERS

LUXARDO MARASCHINO LIQUEUR

SPARKLING WINE

THE 12-BOTTLE BAR

GIN

If you only buy one gin, make it a classic London dry – as this is the style that works best in the greatest number of cocktails.

Beefeater is excellent value, with crisp, clean juniper and citrus notes that shine in mixed drinks.

Tanqueray, which contains no citrus, has a much more spicy, dry bite. A classy, broad-shouldered London dry for mixing old-school stiffeners.

Plymouth Gin is made with sweet, rather than bitter, orange and more mellow, rootsy botanicals that make it softer and more elegant. It is especially good in more nuanced drinks such as Aviations and Martinis.

Hepple is distilled with rain-drenched botanicals foraged on the Northumbrian moors. Complex but fresh, and juniper-forward, it's a first-rate cocktail gin.

Strength-wise, aim for something in the 40–47% abv (alcohol by volume) range – any stronger tends to be unmanageable; any weaker tends to be bland.

The vermouth I always have in the fridge for Martinis is the French brand Noilly Prat Dry. Made in the south of France from oak-aged white wines, herbs, spices and citrus, this light-gold vermouth has a slightly nuttier, more saline character than many of its peers. And it's that appetising quality that's made it a favourite of Martini drinkers around the world for more than 100 years.

Another good vermouth in this more savoury vein is La Copa Blanco Extra Seco by sherry producer González Byass – based on fino sherry, it has a slightly salty tang.

Fresher and perhaps more 'pretty' is the Dry from French house Dolin – a classic Chambéry vermouth made from white Savoie wines and herbs picked in the Alps.

It might not be the trendiest choice but Martini & Rossi's red vermouth is a really solid buy – lighter and drier than many red vermouths, it's extremely versatile. Especially suited to spritzy and white-spirit drinks such as Americanos and Negronis.

For a few extra quid, you could get the more upmarket Martini Riserva Speciale Rubino – a traditional Turin-style vermouth with bigger, more complex flavours that work well in whiskey drinks.

I'm also a big fan of the barbera-based *rosso* by Chazalettes. It's twice the price of Martini but arguably twice as interesting, with lively red and black fruit, woody spice and sage-y wormwood notes that are great in cocktails or just neat, on ice.

A note on terminology *Vermouth terminology is confusing, to say the least. Red, or* rosso, *vermouth is often referred to in cocktail guides as 'sweet' or 'Italian' vermouth – both terms that are pretty unhelpful. 'Sweet' makes no sense because if you go on sugar content, white vermouth (see below) is the sweetest style of all. 'Italian' is a nonsense too, these days, because red vermouth is made all over the world. In this book I call this vermouth 'red'. Dry vermouth – sometimes called 'French' vermouth – 'dry'. And sweet white, or 'bianco' vermouth, I refer to as 'white'.*

BOURBON OR RYE WHISKEY

You must have an American whiskey, of course – but should it be bourbon or rye?

All the real classics – the Old Fashioned, the Manhattan and the Sazerac – would have originally been made with rye, as this was the style of whiskey that prevailed in the States up until Prohibition. Peppery, spicy and flavoursome, rye whiskey is wonderful stuff. Pikesville and Sazerac Straight Rye both make a good Manhattan. Wild Turkey Rye is also splendidly cranky.

Bourbon, which is based on corn, tends to be sweeter, easier-sipping. Its notes of caramel, vanilla, tobacco and baking spices play more nicely with other things. Buffalo Trace and Woodford Reserve are both excellent all-rounders. Further up the scale you've also got Michter's Bourbon and Eagle Rare – both would make a really five-star Old Fashioned. The strength of American whiskies can vary considerably – so keep an eye on the abv. The recipes in this book work best with whiskies in the 40–47% abv range.

CAMPARI

Oft-imitated, but never bettered, this bittersweet Italian liqueur is the gateway to a multitude of delicious aperitivi. But it's also great in a simple highball with tonic, soda or grapefruit juice. My kitchen is never without it.

COGNAC

Younger VS and VSOP cognacs tend to be much fruitier and more supple – which is what you want when you're making a brandy drink. H by Hine and Rémy Martin VSOP are both excellent in cocktails. I also love pretty much anything by Frapin.

My ideal drinks cabinet would contain two rums: a light, dry rum for making Daiquiris and Mojitos, and a darker, more mature rum for punches and slow-stirred cocktails. If you can only run to one, choose on the basis of what you like to drink.

Light, dry rum originated in Cuba, and was made famous by Bacardi and Havana Club. My favourite example is the pale gold Havana Club 3yo – grassy, citrusy and ever-so-slightly medicinal, it makes a superlative Daiquiri. Slightly rounder and sweeter is Plantation 3 Stars, a blend of white rums from across the Caribbean that's so smooth you could sip it neat.

When it comes to amber mixing rums, the Jamaican distillery Appleton is queen – its fruity, funky pot-still spirits give real sass to punches and cocktails. Barbados's Foursquare and Mount Gay distilleries, and the Guyanese distillery El Dorado, also make excellent rums that run the gamut from cheap and cheerful to serious *digestifs*.

A good tequila should have polish – but it shouldn't be too clean. You want to taste the peculiar mix of mineral, citrus and vegetal notes that's so particular to the agave plant.

Steer clear of inferior mixto varieties and go for an unaged *blanco* or lightly aged *reposado* tequila that's made from 100% Blue Weber agave (it will usually say on the label).

Ocho and Tapatio are two tequilas that combine freshness with great character – both are made at the same distillery in the red-dust highlands of Jalisco. Olmeca Altos, which was co-created by bartender and agave aficionado Henry Besant, is also good.

It's harder to recommend a mezcal as the range of styles is so great. And quite frankly, if you're a mezcal drinker, you probably already know what you like anyway.

TRIPLE SEC

Cointreau is the most famous example of this crystal-clear orange liqueur. But Merlet also makes a triple sec called Trois Citrus that's wonderfully zesty. Triple sec overlaps with orange curaçao, an orange liqueur that is brandy-based – at a pinch it can often be used as a (rather lighter) substitute. (**See** *Orange curaçao – p.22.*)

COCKTAIL BITTERS

Angostura is the bitters brand you'll see behind most bars. But if I was only allowed one variety of bitters, I'd go for orange bitters as they're much more versatile: they work in all the whiskey drinks that call for classic Angostura, but also bring an extra lift to many white-spirit drinks: Margaritas, Daiquiris, Punches, Gimlets and Martinis. They're good in tonic and cola and even in hot water.

Angostura Orange Bitters are big on marmaladey spice; Bitter Truth Orange bitters have a zesty freshness more like orange peel; Regans' Orange Bitters taste almost like Campari.

Of course, as you've probably guessed, I don't own just one bottle of bitters – I own lots: cherry-red Peychaud's Bitters from New Orleans (**see** *Expanding the Repertoire –p.22*) and Bittermens bitters with grapefruit and hops; paper-wrapped walnut bitters from Fee Brothers; cocoa bitters and celery bitters and *shiso* bitters from Japan. Each one of these potent tinctures brings something different to a drink. A fun and easy way to instantly expand your cocktail repertoire.

LUXARDO MARASCHINO LIQUEUR

Distilled in Torreglia from the stones, bark and leaves of the sour marasca cherry, this transparent liqueur has a sweet, almondy scent as intoxicating as that of a magic marker. It's key to vintage classics including the Aviation and the Last Word but it can also be used in place of sugar syrup to make virtually any cocktail a bit more interesting. There are other brands of maraschino but Luxardo's is by far the best – one instance where I will accept no substitutes.

SPARKLING WINE

Using your best vintage champagne in a cocktail won't make it taste better – in fact, it will almost certainly make it worse. What you want when you're mixing is a wine that's youthful and fresh and easy-going – that doesn't need to be the star of the show.

Just about any sparkling wine will work in a cocktail as long as it's not too oaky: prosecco, crémant, English sparkling, champagne. It really boils down to what you've got open.

When it comes to still wine you can even get away with using something that's a teensy bit over the hill. You know that open bottle of wine you've got hanging around that's not quite nice enough to drink any more, but not yet bad enough to throw away? That wine is probably perfect.

A NOTE ON STORING SPIRITS, LIQUEURS & APERITIFS

———

Spirits and liqueurs will go on tasting better, for longer, if they're stored out of direct light and in a place where the temperature doesn't fluctuate too much. A cool, dark cupboard is perfect. On top of the tumble dryer, in the glare of the midday sun, is not.

Contrary to what you may have heard, spirits do deteriorate once opened. And as the amount of oxygen in the bottle increases, the rate of decline speeds up. It's a process that takes years, rather than months. But it can sneak up on you. Once a bottle of spirits is less than a quarter full, it's time to finish up.

Wine-based aperitifs such as vermouth oxidise faster than spirits, but you can slow that process down by keeping open bottles in the fridge. An open bottle, kept well chilled, should go on tasting its best for two to three months (and will remain perfectly drinkable, quite frankly, for several months after that).

EXPANDING THE REPERTOIRE

———

ABSINTHE – Cocktails don't call for absinthe that often, but when they do, there's no getting round it. On the upside, you rarely need more than a few drops, so a single bottle lasts for ages. Decanting your absinthe into a little bottle with a dropper will make dispensing small amounts much easier. I use Pernod Absinthe.

COCCHI AMERICANO – This golden, wine-based aperitif is a bit like vermouth but it's bittered with quinine rather than wormwood. A rather rarified ingredient but essential to a few great classics, including the Corpse Reviver No.2 (**see** *The Gin Sour – p.87*) and the Martini Vesper (**see** *The Martini – p.90*). Also delicious on ice, with a dash of soda or tonic. Store in the fridge.

COFFEE LIQUEUR – By far the best coffee liqueur I've tasted is the Australian brand Mr Black – it has a serious roasty hit and comes in single-origin varieties too.

DRY SHERRY – Sherry is great for bringing a savoury tang to sours and aperitifs – but it's also the base for a few great classics in its own right. La Gitana Manzanilla or Tio Pepe Fino are both good for mixing.

ORANGE CURAÇAO – Orange curaçao is an orange liqueur in a similar vein to triple sec – but it's one that's based on brandy so it has more weight and depth. Two well-known varieties are Grand Marnier and Pierre Ferrand Curaçao. If you don't have orange curaçao, you can usually sub in triple sec – you may just find the resulting drink doesn't have quite the same gravitas.

ORGEAT – I know some energetic souls who make this non-alcoholic almond syrup from scratch, but Monin Orgeat does the job for me. Essential to a Mai Tai.

PEATED SCOTCH WHISKY – Really great Scotch whisky cocktails are few and far between, but a peated Scotch whisky will add a smoky string to your bow. Johnnie Walker Black Label has a subtle smokiness that works in cocktails short and long. For a more piquant, peaty hit, I love the Islay malt Lagavulin 16yo.

PEYCHAUD'S BITTERS – If you've already got Angostura Bitters and orange bitters, these cherry-red bitters should be your next purchase – if only because they look so nice on the kitchen shelf. Invented in the 1830s in an apothecary in the French Quarter of New Orleans, they are best known as the signature ingredient in the Sazerac.

Milder and sweeter than many bitters, with notes of caraway, spearmint and cinnamon, they can be dispensed pretty liberally into gin sours and whiskey drinks.

VODKA – If you drink a lot of Vodkatinis, the flavoursome Polish rye vodka Belvedere might be worth the investment, but otherwise a good-value brand like Wyborowa or Finlandia do the job just fine.

WHITE VERMOUTH – White – or *bianco*, or *blanco* or *blanc* – vermouth should not be confused with dry vermouth – it's much sweeter, with vanilla and citrus accents. It was a style invented to appeal to women in the early 20th century and ever since has had a rather cheesy reputation, not helped by those 1970s Cinzano ads with Joan Collins. In the right hands, though, it can be very sophisticated, as I hope the recipes in this book prove.

OTHER SPECIALITIES
MENTIONED IN THIS BOOK

———

CALVADOS – Cask-aged fruit brandy from Normandy made from apples and, sometimes, pears.

KUMMEL – Piercingly sweet, colourless caraway liqueur popular in Holland and Germany.

YUZUSHU – Citrussy yellow liqueur made from a blend of sherbetty yuzu fruit, sugar and sake and/or shochu. The Japanese answer to limoncello.

LONDON PRIDE – Tawny amber ale brewed on the banks of the River Thames.

CRÈME DE MÛRE – Blackberry liqueur – the crème de mûre by French distiller Merlet is particularly good.

FERNET-BRANCA – Pitch black, face-puckeringly bitter Italian *digestivo* with a cooling minty finish.

AQUAVIT – Scandinavian botanical spirit characterised by bright anise and herbaceous notes. Try the Norwegian brand Nuet.

SUZE – Bittersweet, bright yellow gentian liqueur from France that can be used in a similar way to Campari.

CYNAR – Woody, smoky-sweet Italian amaro made from artichokes – use anywhere you'd use red vermouth.

BÉNÉDICTINE DOM – Highly aromatic monastic liqueur distilled from 27 different herbs and spices.

DRAMBUIE – Warming Scotch whisky liqueur flavoured with spices, herbs and heather honey.

AMARETTO – Almond-flavoured Italian liqueur traditionally – but not always – made from almonds. Saliza Amaretto is the real deal.

GINGER LIQUEUR – The King's Ginger, originally created for King Edward VII, has a nice kick to it. If you don't have liqueur, you can sub with ginger cordial and an extra dash of sugar syrup.

GREEN CHARTREUSE – Jade green liqueur with a kaleidoscope of herbaceous flavours. Great for seasoning lime sours and as a sub for absinthe in many whiskey drinks.

WHITE PORT – The lighter, drier cousin of ruby port – great in a highball with tonic.

NON-ALCOHOLIC INGREDIENTS

COCKTAIL CHERRIES – The gold standard are the glossy black maraschino cherries by Italian distiller Luxardo. For more on cherries **see** *The Garnish – p.60.*

COFFEE – Save your esoteric, single-origin coffees for elevenses – what you want for cocktails is a straightforward ground coffee (or espresso) on the more nutty/chocolatey side.

CREAM – There are only two drinks in this book that call for cream and in both cases it's single (light).

EGG WHITE – For whiskey sours and fizzes. Aquafaba, or canned chickpea water, can be used as a vegan substitute. It fluffs up beautifully when shaken, but I find its leguminous pong a bit off-putting.

FRUIT JUICES – The finer aromas and flavours in citrus fruits start to fade as soon as they're juiced. For that reason, citrus juices – and especially lemon and lime juice – should always be freshly squeezed.

If, like me, you don't have a serious juicer, getting hold of things such as good-quality pineapple juice can be a bit more difficult. I've suggested ways round this, but you may have to go shop-bought. Steer clear of long-life nectars and concentrates and go for fresh juices, with bits in, from the chiller cabinet. Tomato juice, in particular, is worth spending money on – Big Tom, Turner Hardy & Co and The Pickle House are three good brands.

GRAPEFRUITS – Pink grapefruit would be my preference as it makes a prettier garnish and has juice that's a little less sharp.

ICE – Crucial – for chapter and verse on this **see** *The Importance of Ice – p.36.*

LEMONS – I don't know how many recipes call for lemons in this book but it's a lot – indispensable.

LIMES – Only slightly less indispensable than lemons.

MILK – Full-fat cow's milk is best for cocktails. Or oat milk, if you're plant-based.

MINT & OTHER HERBS – See *The Garnish – p.61.*

ORANGES – Generally more useful for garnishes and sherbets than the actual juice.

SALT – A flaky salt like Maldon salt will cover all your cocktail needs. For tips on doing a salt rim, **see** *The Garnish – p.66.*

SODA WATER – Any brand will do as long as it's fizzy and cold. Always store in the fridge.

SUGAR & OTHER SWEETENERS – See *Sugar Syrups (and Other Sweeteners) – p.30.*

TEA – Tea is a wonderful ingredient that can bring freshness, flavour, texture and caffeine to cocktails short and long. A really good loose-leaf will make all the difference, especially in short drinks such as the Jasmine Tea Martini. Rare Tea Co, Jing and Postcard Teas are all excellent.

TONIC WATER – I'm a dyed-in-the-wool Schweppes drinker. But if I had to pick a low-cal option, it would be Fever Tree Light. Always buy in small cans or bottles and store in the fridge. Also good with: tequila, Campari, vodka, dry sherry, white port, vermouth (and other wine-based aperitifs) and aquavit.

SUGAR SYRUPS
(& OTHER SWEETENERS)

A huge number of cocktail recipes call for sugar syrup – so I always have some on hand. You can buy ready-made but it's cheaper and quicker to make yourself. If you make it from scratch, it also gives you the option to play around with other kinds of sugars and flavourings.

The 2:1 sugar syrup is a standard formula – and it's the one I've used for all the recipes in this book. I usually make up to half a litre at a time and keep it in a swing-top bottle in the fridge door.

2:1 SUGAR SYRUP

Makes 500ml

500g white caster (superfine) sugar*
250ml water

In a small saucepan, bring the sugar and water to the boil. Turn down the heat and leave to simmer until all the sugar has dissolved (a couple of minutes usually). Take off the heat and leave to cool. Bottle. Stored in the fridge, the syrup should keep for a couple of months.

Or any other type of sugar. A treacly muscovado sugar syrup would be great in an Old Fashioned. Or try sweetening a Daiquiri with a syrup made from golden demerara (light brown sugar).

FLAVOURED SUGAR SYRUPS

Using a flavoured syrup in place of a plain one is one of the easiest ways to give a drink a twist. And there's something really gratifying about making a cocktail with a syrup you've flavoured yourself. Some syrups can be flavoured in less than an hour – others take a bit longer to infuse. But all bring something new to a drink, as I hope The Gimlet chapter in particular proves (**see** *p.134*).

Delicate herbs and flowers such as lemon verbena, tarragon, scented geranium leaves or orange blossom are best-suited to cold infusion – a gentler process that just involves steeping them in 2:1 sugar syrup so that they exhale their scent. Don't be too precious about quantities – if you have more to play with, just stuff it all in. And then leave to infuse for roughly eight hours – or until it reaches a flavour that you like.

Tougher, more fibrous ingredients such as spices, citrus peels, rosehips or ginger need the application of a little heat – but this can be done while making the sugar syrup.

Here are the recipes for some flavoured syrups that feature in this book. All of them make 250ml.

LEMON VERBENA SYRUP

5 handfuls of lemon verbena
250ml of 2:1 sugar syrup

Place the leaves in a jug or Kilner jar, cover with syrup and leave to infuse for eight hours. Strain and bottle. Store in the fridge.

See *Lemon Verbena Tequila Punch – p.158*.

TARRAGON SYRUP

5 handfuls of tarragon
250ml of 2:1 sugar syrup

Place the leaves in a jug or Kilner jar, cover with syrup and leave to infuse for eight hours. Strain and bottle. Store in the fridge.

See *Tarragon Gimlet – p.137*.

BAY LEAF SYRUP

250g sugar

125ml water

4–6 bay leaves

Bring the ingredients to the boil in a small saucepan, turn down the heat and leave to simmer until all the sugar is dissolved. Take off the heat and leave to cool. Strain and bottle. Store in the fridge.

See *Apple & Bay Leaf Sour – p.145.*

ROSEHIP SYRUP

250g sugar

125ml water

2 handfuls cleaned, chopped rosehips (dog roses are especially fragrant)

Bring the ingredients to the boil in a small saucepan, turn down the heat and leave to simmer until all the sugar is dissolved. Take off the heat and leave to cool. Strain and bottle. Store in the fridge.

See *Rosehip Gimlet –p.138.*

GRAPEFRUIT SYRUP

250g sugar

125ml water

75ml grapefruit juice

Finely grated (shredded) zest of 2 grapefruits

Bring the ingredients to the boil in a small saucepan, turn down the heat and leave to simmer until all the sugar is dissolved. Take off the heat and leave to cool. Strain and bottle. Store in the fridge.

See *Grapefruit Gimlet – p.136.*

GINGER SYRUP

250g sugar

125ml water

125g peeled, finely chopped root ginger

Bring the ingredients to the boil in a small saucepan, turn down the heat and leave to simmer until all the sugar is dissolved. Take off the heat and leave to cool. Strain and bottle. Store in the fridge.

See *Shaky Pete's Ginger Brew – p.168.*

SHERBETS

In Georgian times punches were often sweetened with loaf sugar scented with lemon peel – a preparation known as an *oleo saccharum*, or what we might call a sherbet. Zesty, fragrant and slightly bitter, a sherbet can make even the simplest sour absolutely dazzle.

Lemon, blood orange, grapefruit, yuzu (or even a mix) all make very good sherbets. If the skin is very bitter, just add a bit more sugar.

Ideally, a sherbet should be prepared the night before, so the zest has the maximum time to infuse. But you can busk an instant one by simply muddling ribbons of peel with sugar.

ORANGE & LEMON SHERBET

Makes 100g or enough for a punch that serves 12

2 lemons
2 oranges
100g caster (superfine) sugar
100ml mix of lemon and orange juice

Zest the lemons and oranges with a speed peeler, taking as little of the pith as possible. Pack the peels tightly in a jar with the sugar and leave for several hours to infuse (overnight, ideally). On the day, tip the sherbet, peels and all, into the appointed punch bowl, add the citrus juice and stir to dissolve the sugar. Then add the other punch ingredients.

See *Tequila and Lemon Verbena Punch – p.158.*

OTHER TYPES OF SWEETENER

HONEY SYRUP – especially good with rum. Just mix honey 2:1 with hot water and leave to cool.

AGAVE SYRUP – more intensely sweet than normal sugar syrup, so you may need less.

MAPLE SYRUP – particularly suited to whiskey cocktails.

LIQUEURS – You can often use Luxardo Maraschino Liqueur or triple sec wholly or partly in place of sugar to give a drink a little extra something. (And vice versa – you can usually use sugar syrup in place of maraschino or triple sec in an emergency.) Liqueurs are slightly less sweet than sugar syrup, so you may need to compensate by adding 5–10ml extra per serve.

THE IMPORTANCE OF ICE

The most common mistake home mixologists make is that they don't use enough ice: for shaking, for stirring, for chilling, for serving. For every stage in mixing a drink.

Ice is important, first and foremost, because it lowers the temperature of the ingredients. This brightens citrus, tempers sweetness, preserves fizz – it gets a cocktail up on its toes.

Ice also imparts dilution, which really helps a drink breathe. It creates a bridge between warring ingredients and cools the heat of the alcohol.

A well-iced drink is mouthwatering to look at. It's more exciting to touch. It even sounds better – is there any sweeter music on a summer evening than the clink of a G&T?

So from now on please resolve, always, to use at least five cubes per drink. And whether you're shaking, stirring or serving, try to use fresh ice, if possible, each time.

I realise this may sound extravagant. But the more ice you use – and the bigger and colder those cubes are – the slower it will melt. Which means your drink will stay colder for longer, without getting too diluted.

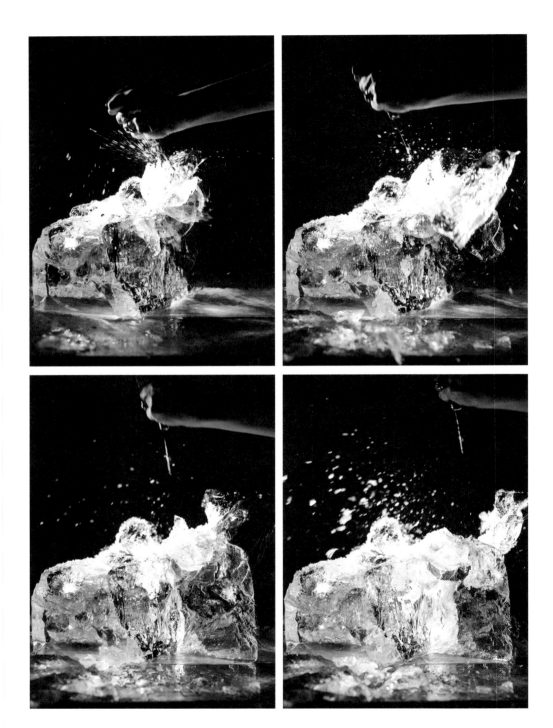

MAKING ICE

ICE CUBES – The bigger the better when it comes to ice cubes – aim for 3cm^3. Most domestic ice trays are not up to the job but the Bar Original Silicone Jumbo Ice Tray is an exception – it's flexible, stackable, unbreakable and makes 32 cubes of a generous size. I always have two of these on the go. For large gatherings I'll also buy cubes by the bag.

ICE BLOCKS – Slow-melting iceblocks are great for punches and big sharing drinks, which need to be kept cold over a long period of time. Simply fill up an old Tupperware box or ice-cream tub with water and freeze.

ICEBERGS – A Negroni or an Old Fashioned looks stunning over a jagged hunk of ice. Place an ice block (see above) on a dish towel so it doesn't slip and hack it to bits with a sharp implement and a mallet. The more irregular the bergs are, the better. I always have a bag of these in the freezer.

CRACKED ICE – A bit more gnarly than cubed ice, but not as high maintenance as crushed ice. Great for long, cool drinks such as Cobblers and Juleps. Just wrap some cubes in a dish towel and give them a quick wallop with a rolling pin.

CRUSHED ICE – Crushed ice is laborious to make, messy to work with and melts impossibly fast. And it's very rarely essential – the only recipe in this book that really calls for it is the Bramble (**see** *The Gin Sour – p.86*).

CRYSTAL-CLEAR ICE – Cloudy ice is caused by air bubbles trapped in the ice, rather than impurities in the water. So boiling or purifying your water first won't give you clearer ice, I'm afraid. For really stunning ice, I go to a specialist supplier like Ice Studio, which does spheres, blocks and ingots so clear you can read a book through them.

EQUIPMENT

BAR TOOLS

It's perfectly possible to make good cocktails without any specialist equipment. But the results will taste better – and probably be more fun to make – if you have a few dedicated tools.

ESSENTIAL

JIGGER

Just 5ml (a teaspoon) is sometimes all that stands between a cocktail that's sublime, and one that falls flat on its face – so having a tool that measures liquids accurately is crucial.

You'll probably be familiar with those stainless steel, nip-waisted jiggers that have a 50ml/2oz/double measure at one end and a 25ml/1oz/single measure at the other. Perhaps you even own one. In which case you'll know that they're great for measuring a single or double shot – but not much good for measuring anything in between.

I much prefer the Easy Jigger by cocktail supremo Simon Difford. This funnel-shaped, plastic jigger measures in increments from 1.25ml to 60ml (and their equivalents in fl oz) and, importantly, has the numbers on the inside so the level is easier to read. It also has a big foot on the bottom that means you can leave it hanging upside down on the edge of the mixing glass while sticky syrups and liqueurs ooze out. A great piece of kit, designed by a pro.

BOSTON SHAKER & HAWTHORNE STRAINER

Three-piece shakers look pretty, but for sheer practicality you can't beat a Boston – the two-piece glass-and-tin shaker used by most bartenders. Bostons are cheap, easy to use, easy to clean and virtually indestructible – I've been using the same one now for more than 15 years and it's still going strong.

The ingredients go in the glass half, and the ice goes in the tin – then the two halves fit together to make a shaker that's long enough to make two drinks at a time. If you're using a Boston, you will also need a Hawthorne strainer, a tennis racquet-shaped tool that fits over the mouth of the tin and holds back the ice as you pour.

The glass half also doubles as a mixing glass for stirred drinks (and when you're not making cocktails, it's a vase, pint glass and breadstick holder, too).

JUICER

A regular juicer is fine, but if you plan on making a lot of drinks with limes – which tend to be on the firm side – I'd recommend getting a citrus press (sometimes known as a Mexican Elbow), which works a bit like a garlic crusher, and makes the whole process of squeezing fruit a lot easier. The lime half should be placed in the squeezer cut side down (you can always flip it round and squeeze the other way for more oils after, if you wish).

ICE TRAY

I have strong views on this. **See** *Making Ice – p. 39*.

NICE TO HAVE

LONG-HANDLED BARSPOON

You can stir a drink with anything – a spoon, a chopstick, a knife. But an elegant, long-handled barspoon will make the whole experience much more pleasurable. The best end of the spoon for stirring, counterintuitively, is actually the end without the spoon on it (**see** *Techniques* – p.53). The spoon itself can be used for scooping garnishes and measuring increments of 5ml.

COCKTAIL PICKS

I have a set of 12 razor-sharp stainless steel cocktail picks that I bought for a tenner and use all the time for spearing cherries and olives and bending twists into strange shapes. They instantly make any cocktail look much more pro.

OTHER THINGS YOU MAY HAVE ALREADY

Corkscrew/bottle opener

Knife

Chopping board

Speed peeler
– for cutting twists

Fine strainer
– for double-straining drinks

Straws *– reusable or paper, preferably*

Rolling pin and dish towel *– for crushing ice*

Tupperware *– for making block ice/storing herbs, etc.*

Blender *– Vitamix and NutriBullet are two brands tough enough to blitz ice*

Dropper bottle
– for dropper-ing tinctures and bitters

Pestle and mortar
– for muddling ingredients

Swing-top bottles, Kilner jars or old jam jars *– for making and storing syrups and infusions*

Fruit bowl/mixing bowl *– for punches*

Ladle *– for serving punches. Preferably one with a spout-like taper at either end*

Measuring jugs
– for batching cocktails

Large jug
– for punches and cups

GLASSWARE

I have too much glassware – so much, in fact, that when something gets smashed it comes as a bit of a relief. I've got gilt-edged coupes from a New York flea market and wobbly Japanese tumblers designed to look like flowing water; Georgian-style goblets and retro Nick & Nora coupes; cut-glass crystal tumblers and £1 rocks glasses from the pound shop; shiny metal julep tins and long-stemmed liqueur glasses that belonged to my gran.

Choosing which glass to use is part of the pleasure for me – each one gives the drink a different character. But you could easily get by with just three types of glass – and maybe even two.

COCKTAIL GLASS

A stemmed cocktail glass is essential for any cocktail that's served 'up' (without ice); the stem prevents the drink from being warmed by the drinker's hand.

I prefer the curvaceous coupe to the Y-shaped variety – it looks more timeless and it just feels nicer to use. It's often claimed the coupe was based on the shape of Marie Antoinette's left breast. This is a myth, sadly, but the frisson lives on.

The problem with most cocktail glasses is that they are far too big – so the drink ends up tepid (and you end up completely smashed) before you're even halfway through.

Always err on the small side when choosing a cocktail glass: for short, concentrated drinks like Martinis and Manhattans, a dainty 120ml coupe is ideal.

For sours, frozen drinks and champagne cocktails, you may want a slightly more generous glass in the 180–200ml region. (Pretty much any cocktail that calls for a flute will also work in a coupe, by the way.)

If you only buy one glass, however, make it the 150ml Nick & Nora – a classic design that elegantly manages to accommodate cocktails both big and small.

ROCKS GLASS

This is the only other glass I'd consider essential. Go for something capacious enough to take a nice big hunk of ice.

HIGHBALL

You can get away with serving spirit and mixer drinks in a rocks glass – so a highball is not essential. But a long, tall glass is nice to have for G&Ts and ice-laden cocktails that come with a straw, such as sherry Cobblers and Mojitos. You probably already own something like this, anyway.

CHILLING GLASSWARE

A cocktail tastes a hundred thousand times better if it's served in a glass that's really cold. So always give glassware a blast in the freezer for a couple of minutes before you use it (I have a couple of glasses permanently on standby in the freezer). If you're out of freezer space, stick your glassware in the fridge, or fill it up with ice cubes and water to chill while you're mixing the drink. Freezing your mixing glass before you use it is another good way to give your Martini the edge.

TECHNIQUES

SHAKING, STIRRING
& SO ON

SHAKE

Commonly reserved for cocktails containing fruit juice, eggs or dairy, which require more energetic mixing. But also good for any drink that suits being a bit more dilute.

Let's assume you're using a Boston shaker:

Put your ingredients in the glass half of the shaker and fill the tin two-thirds full with ice. Insert the glass into the tin until the two halves make a seal. Strengthen the seal by giving the base of the tin a little tap on the table.

Hold the shaker at shoulder height and shake really hard for between 10 and 15 seconds. (Spectators might want to politely look away at this point.)

The ideal shaking time will vary from drink to drink, but keep going until there's frost on the outside of the tin. The sound of the ice is also a useful indicator – if it goes from clunky to jingly then it's definitely time to stop.

Hold the shaker tin-end downwards and separate the two halves. If they won't budge, give the shaker a gentle tap on the table at the point where glass and tin meet, to break the seal.

Taste and adjust if necessary. Then fit the Hawthorne strainer over the mouth of the tin and pour.

STIR

Commonly reserved for short, strong cocktails that suit being silky and concentrated. Elegant stirring takes a bit of practice – but it's much easier, and more fun, with a long-handled barspoon (**see** *Equipment – p.46*).

Fill the mixing glass two-thirds with ice and add your ingredients. Insert the non-spoon end of the barspoon (or other straight tool) in among the ice cubes and give them a nudge so they start spinning round. Keep the ice spinning in a silent, fluid motion for between 20 and 30 seconds. Stop, taste, adjust and stir some more, if necessary. Then fit the Hawthorne strainer over the mouth of the mixing glass and pour.

When it comes to making stirred drinks that are served on the rocks, such as Negronis and Old Fashioneds, you have the choice of either stirring the drink in a mixing glass and then straining it over fresh ice, or simply stirring it in the glass it's destined to be served in. If I was working at The Savoy, I'd do the former. But in reality I generally do the latter, and then just top the drink up with a few extra ice cubes once it's stirred.

MUDDLE

Crushing, pressing or lightly bruising ingredients in the bottom of a vessel to release the aromas and flavours. On the whole, people tend to over-muddle rather than under-muddle, resulting in herbs or fruits that are bruised and mushy. So if in doubt, go easy – think of it as gentle pressing rather than full-on pounding. It's possible to buy dedicated cocktail muddlers but a pestle or the end of a rolling pin will do the job just as well.

STRAIN

Pouring a cocktail through a strainer, so that the ice and any other detritus (peels, herbs etc) are left behind in the shaker. The best tool for doing this is a Hawthorne strainer (**see** *Equipment – p.43*) as it fits neatly over the mouth of most mixing/shaking vessels. With a bit of practice you can do this one-handed, by holding the glass between your thumb and pinky and the Hawthorne down, over the top, with your index and middle finger. You'll definitely need to be able do this if you want to double-strain (see below).

DOUBLE-STRAIN

Straining a cocktail through a Hawthorne (or other strainer) and a fine strainer too, to make it extra-clarified. Ideally this should be done in one fell swoop, with the Hawthorne-topped shaker in one hand and the fine strainer underneath.

CHURN

Stirring ingredients through crushed or cracked ice. To prevent ice going everywhere and making a mess, start with a glass that's only two-thirds full of crushed ice. Add half your ingredients, churn (with a clean hand placed lightly over the top of the glass to stop the ice escaping) then add more ice, the rest of the ingredients and churn a bit more. Once the drink is thoroughly mixed, you can finish it with a cap of crushed ice so it looks smart.

BUILD

What you do with a G&T – basically bar-speak for 'put-it-all-in-a-glass-together'.

TWIST

A piece of citrus peel, used to scent the drink. For more on this **see** *The Garnish – p.59*.

UP

Served without ice, in a stemmed cocktail glass.

OVER ICE/ON THE ROCKS

Served over ice – but you knew that already, didn't you?

FROZEN

A slushie-style cocktail that's been blitzed with ice. Make
sure you smash your ice up a bit first before adding it to the
blender – if you just throw in a big hunk you'll end up with
a lumpy, uneven drink, and a broken blender too. A really
hardcore blender will make your life much easier – Vitamix and
NutriBullet are both good brands.

Frozen cocktails contain a lot more dilution than normal ones,
so they need a higher proportion of sweet and sour in the mix.
All the frozen recipes in this book already take this into account
but if you're inventing one from scratch, adjust the 4:2:1 sour
formula to something more like 5:3:2.

SOME USEFUL MEASUREMENTS

25ml = 1 shot

50ml = 2 shots

1fl oz = 30ml

1 average lemon = approx. 50ml juice

1 average lime = approx. 25ml juice

1 teaspoon = approx. 5ml

Allow at least five ice cubes per drink for serving,
shaking and stirring

A NOTE ON MAKING ADJUSTMENTS

However accurate a recipe is, and however carefully you follow it, there will be times when it inevitably needs a tweak to accommodate the ripeness of your lemons, or the style of gin you're using, or just to suit your own personal taste. Try not to fear it – embrace it! All the best bartenders taste and adjust. The worst that can happen, if it all goes wrong, is you have to pour a cocktail down the sink.

When assessing a cocktail, ask yourself: is it balanced? Are sweet, sour and bitter in harmony? What is the texture and intensity like: is it too weak or too syrupy?

TOO SOUR: add more sweetness – a dash of sugar syrup or liqueur.

TOO SWEET: add more sour/citrus. Or if it's a drink with no sour in it, add more bitter(s). If the drink is very sweet and syrupy, it may also need more dilution.

TOO BITTER: add more dilution and/or sweet.

TOO STRONG: stir or shake for longer, or add a drop more water.

TOO WEAK: add more of everything, but particularly booze. Sugar can also be very good for giving a drink more weight and push.

It's always wise to have a little extra sugar syrup, citrus, bitters and water/ice on hand when mixing a cocktail – because most problems can usually be fixed with one of these.

RUNNING ORDER FOR MAKING A

COCKTAIL

A cocktail's window of perfection is fleeting – so you need to work at speed.
You'll find the whole thing easier if you have a bit of a routine.

1. PUT GLASS IN THE FREEZER

2. ASSEMBLE TOOLS AND LOCATE ICE
(BUT LEAVE ICE IN THE FREEZER FOR NOW)

3. ASSEMBLE AND PREP INGREDIENTS
(E.G. JUICE LEMONS AND SEPARATE EGG WHITES)

4. PREP GARNISH AND PUT IT ON STANDBY

5. IF IT'S A SHAKEN DRINK: MEASURE INGREDIENTS
INTO THE MIXING GLASS (NO ICE)

You can proceed at a leisurely pace up to this point.
But once the ice is out of the freezer, time is of the essence.

6. IF IT'S A SHAKEN DRINK:
CHARGE THE TIN WITH ICE AND SHAKE

7. IF IT'S A STIRRED DRINK:
CHARGE THE MIXING GLASS WITH ICE,
ADD THE INGREDIENTS AND STIR

8. TASTE AND ADJUST IF NECESSARY

9. REMOVE GLASS FROM THE FREEZER

10. POUR THE DRINK IMMEDIATELY,
GARNISH AND ENJOY

THE GARNISH

Some garnishes add a pop of colour. Others add aroma or taste. The best ones – as you'll know if you've ever put a mint-topped Julep to your lips – are the ones that do all three. Occasionally, a garnish can tell a story, or even make you laugh. There's definitely a time and a place for a bacon rasher or an origami bird.

In the main, though, keep it simple – and add it with élan. The twist on the Manhattan, the olive in the spritz; it's what makes the whole thing dance.

LEMONS, ORANGES & OTHER CITRUS FRUIT

You have two options when it comes to the citrus garnish: the twist or the slice. The twist gives you more of the fragrance, the slice gives you more of the juice. Either way, you'll get much better results if you use fruit with skin that's really taut and fresh – and unwaxed, preferably.

TWIST

A sherbetty twist of lemon, orange or grapefruit peel can completely light up a drink – it's the garnish I use the most, by far.

With a speed-peeler or sharp knife, cut a thumb-sized piece of peel (if the raggedy edges are not to your liking, you can always tidy them up after). Hold the peel shiny-side down over the drink and give it a pinch to express the oils. Anoint the rim of the glass with the peel and then either drop it into the drink or discard as you wish.

If your cocktail is very dainty, a small disc of zest, planed off the edge of the fruit, may work better than a big strip. It's obviously easier if you cut the twist before you juice the fruit.

If you find yourself left with a little pile of offcuts after the first drink, don't throw them away. Pile them on to the next cocktail in a pretty tangle – lemon, orange, grapefruit, all jumbled up together. Or throw them in the shaker, along with the other ingredients, to give the next drink some extra zing.

SLICE

When cutting a slice or a wedge or a wheel, be generous, and cut at right angles to the ends of the fruit – this will produce a wedge that looks smarter, with a lot less pith.

CHERRIES

There are days, or nights, when only a neon-pink cocktail cherry will do – and then I reach for the Opies, which are as fabulously plastic as they come.

In my more discerning moments, I prefer the glossy black maraschino cherries by Luxardo. Made by steeping sour marasca cherries in a heavy cherry juice syrup (but no booze), they are sticky, sweet and sour. It's impossible to have just one. A spoonful of the syrup is also excellent in a Manhattan.

HERBS

MINT – the smell of fresh mint can turn heads at 20 paces. However many times I use it, its wonderful scent takes me by surprise.

When selecting your mint sprig, go big. A mean little sprig just looks sad. Pick off any leaves that are damaged or brown. And before you put it in the drink, give it a sharp clap between your palms to really amp up the scent.

If the sprig is destined for a drink in a tall glass, leave a few inches of bare stalk on it. This can then be tucked down inside and helps the mint stand proud.

Revive tired-looking mint by plunging it into iced water for ten minutes or so. Always store mint – and other herbs – in the fridge door in a container or bag that allows the air to circulate.

Mint is a brute in the garden, but its leaves are quite delicate. Over-zealous muddling can quickly turn them bitter and brown. So I prefer to shake my Mojitos, mint and all. Or just stir whole leaves through the drink – but give them an all-important smack first.

BASIL – great in and on sours and as a garnish for fruity red-berry drinks.

LEMON VERBENA – a wonderful starburst of sherbetty citrus fragrance. Use anywhere you'd use a lemon twist or mint. Also makes a lovely syrup.

ROSEMARY – good in a G&T or paired with orange or grapefruit. Go easy as its scent is quite strong.

DILL & FENNEL – the cool, green anise notes are great in gin drinks such as G&Ts and Martinis.

THYME – nice in a G&T and also good with stone fruit and citrus flavours.

FIG LEAVES – the leaves' opulent, coconutty green perfume is at its best in late summer/early autumn.

If it works well on the drink, it's probably good in the drink as well – next time you make a sour, try chucking a sprig or two of herbs in the shaker, along with the other ingredients.

FLOWERS

A well-placed flower can make a drink look incredibly glamorous – and many of the edible varieties are easy to grow in a hanging basket or pot (some types of flowers are not safe to eat, though, so do be sure what you've got before you stick it in your punch).

Flowers should be picked in the cool of the morning, when the blooms are at their best. Then lay them out in a Tupperware box lined with a piece of damp paper towel. Stored in the fridge like this, they should keep for 48 hours.

LAVENDER – juniper and lavender are a great match. Try garnishing a G&T with a few lavender heads, or shake some with an Aviation (**see** *The Gin Sour – p.84*).

NASTURTIUMS – vibrant red, orange and yellow flowers with a peppery taste and a subtle fragrance. Super easy to grow and great for adding a pop of colour to drinks of all sorts.

VIOLAS & PANSIES – these velvety little blooms don't contribute a huge amount in the way of flavour, but they look absolutely charming.

BORAGE – starry blue flowers with a cucumber-y flavour; the traditional choice for Pimm's and summery punches.

OLIVES & PICKLES

The perfect cocktail olive, in my book, is a fat, green Nocellara olive. And I like it with the stone left in. I don't think a cocktail should be tainted by olives stuffed with anchovies or chilli peppers or blue cheese.

Olives are good in a Martini. And they're also amazing in a bittersweet spritz. Order a *spritz al bitter* in Venice and it will often come with an olive and a citrus slice.

Brined olives add saltiness to a cocktail. Pickles, by contrast, add a vinegar tang. Sweet-and-sour silverskin onions are the hallmark of the Gibson. Caperberries can be good in a Martini, too.

If you like the taste of the juice your pickles or olives come in, throw a teaspoon of that in the mixing glass as well. And always serve the resulting cocktail with a few extra pickles or olives on the side.

SALT RIMS & OTHER SEASONINGS

Salt rims can be spiced up in all kinds of ways to make a drink like a Margarita or a Bloody Mary more interesting. But let's start with a classic salt rim – best done with a flaky variety such as Maldon salt.

Make a little heap of salt on a saucer. Run a wedge of lime around the lip of your glass to wet it. Hold the glass at right angles to the saucer and gently dab the edge of the glass in the salt to give it a light coating. Keep dabbing and turning the glass until you're happy with the effect. A good idea is to only salt half the glass, so people have the choice of with-or-without.

Once you've mastered the basic salt rim, you can go a bit more off-piste: try pink Himalayan salt, black lava salt or *sal de gusano* (a blend of salt, roasted agave worms and smoked chillies that's often served with mezcal in Mexico).

You could add in some fiery spices – on page 124 you'll find a Margarita edged with Japanese shichimi. A Bloody Mary edged with a mix of salt, pepper and celery salt (and shichimi!) is also really good (**see** *16 More Drinks – p.160*).

NUTMEG

In the 18th and 19th centuries, hot and cold drinks were often garnished with a grating of nutmeg. Its warm, woody flavour and sweet fragrance is lovely on creamy drinks such as White Russians and Irish Coffees. But it's also surprisingly good on punches – in this book you'll find it on the sangria-like Badminton Punch (**see** *Punches & Cups – p.157*), a favourite of Charles Dickens.

COCKTAIL ESSENCES

When fresh citrus is in short supply, I'll often use the sprayable citrus essences by Linden Leaf distillery in Cambridge. Available in lemon, orange, grapefruit and yuzu, they do the same job as a twist – great for spritzing on Martinis and G&Ts. The Tuscan company Santa Bianca also does a wonderful range of sprayable essences that include grapefruit and basil, cedarwood, jasmine and damask rose.

BATCHING & BOTTLING

Not all cocktails and mixed drinks have to be made *à la minute* – quite a few can also be batched or bottled in advance. Especially useful if you're throwing a party.

BATCHED COCKTAILS

Batching, or pre-batching, is basically just jargon for mixing a large quantity of one drink ahead of time so that you have less to do when the moment comes. It's a hack that a lot of busy bars use because it makes drinks service quicker, easier and more consistent.

Some drinks – such as punches and bottled cocktails – can be pre-batched in their entirety. Others – especially ones that contain fizzy ingredients – can be pre-batched in part.

A good example of a drink you can pre-batch is the French 75 (**see** *The Gin Sour –p.84*). Instead of assembling the four ingredients – gin, lemon, sugar and champagne – from scratch each time someone wants one, you pre-batch a big jug of the gin, lemon and sugar several hours before the event and put it in the fridge. Once chilled, this pre-mix can then be measured out into lots of glasses at once and topped up with champagne, or even just mixed with champagne in a jug, a bit like a cordial. Pre-batching essentially reduces a recipe that originally required four ingredients to one that requires just two.

The basic recipe stays exactly the same whether you're making drinks for five or 100. The only difference is you need to add 20ml of water, per serve, to the sour pre-mix, to make up for the fact that it's not being shaken or stirred (which would normally provide the dilution). Drinks that are served on the rocks, such as the Negroni Sbagliato, don't need this extra dilution. Nor do drinks such as the Gin Cup, which have a non-alcoholic mixer.

Here are some examples of useful pre-batches
(pre-batched part in italics):

FRENCH 75

Gin + lemon + sugar syrup + water
+
Sparkling wine

NEGRONI SBAGLIATO

Vermouth + Campari
+
Sparkling wine

SENCHA COLLINS

Sencha-infused gin + lemon + sugar syrup
+
Soda water

GIN CUP

Gin + vermouth + triple sec
+
Tonic/lemonade

AIR MAIL

Rum + lime + honey syrup + water
+
Sparkling wine

BOTTLED COCKTAILS

The best cocktails for bottling are short, boozy ones that don't contain any fresh ingredients: Manhattans, Negronis, Martinis, Sazeracs. Stored in the fridge they'll keep very happily for several months, and they make nice presents, too.

Just batch up the cocktail, as normal, but with the addition of an extra 20ml of water per serve. This provides the dilution that would normally be imparted by shaking or stirring, and means the cocktail can then be poured straight from bottle to glass.

Store bottled cocktails in the fridge rather than the freezer (or, below a certain strength, they'll freeze solid). Then give them a blast in the freezer for 30 minutes or so, just before cocktail hour.

Drinks that contain fresh ingredients, such as sours and White Russians, can be bottled too. But they will really only stay at their best for about 24 hours.

Some cocktails that suit more long-term bottling:

MARTINI

MANHATTAN

OLD FASHIONED

BOULEVARDIER

NEGRONI

SAZERAC

HANKY PANKY

USEFUL KIT FOR BATCHING
& BOTTLING

SEVERAL 1.5–2 LITRE MEASURING JUGS

A BIG SPOON FOR MIXING

A FUNNEL

SWING-TOP GLASS BOTTLES

I also have a couple of plastic jerry cans for getting really large amounts of pre-mix from A to B. Unsightly, but extremely practical. I just stash them under the table.

COCKTAILS FOR A CROWD

Mixing a few drinks for an intimate soirée is one thing. Doing cocktails for 50-plus people is quite another. Unless you want to completely lose your mind over it, you need a slightly different approach.

The main problem, in my experience, is that people tend to plan cocktail menus that are massively overambitious. And the result is that they (or sometimes I) end up stuck in the kitchen all night shaking cocktails and smashing ice.

So when it comes to choosing your drinks, be realistic. If you have limited freezer space, for example, then cocktails that require lots of ice, such as Brambles and Cobblers, might be a bad idea. If you've only got one shaker, or a couple of coupes, then give the Espresso Martini a miss.

This doesn't mean cocktails are impossible – it just means you need to choose the right ones.

And the right ones, almost invariably, are the ones that can be partly or wholly made in advance.

Punches and cups are great for parties, as they can be mixed in one fell swoop – **see** *Punches & Cups – p.152* for ideas.

Cocktails that can be bottled or batched are excellent too – **see** *Batching & Bottling – p.68*.

Whatever the size of your gathering, offer three cocktails, absolute max. A short, strong one, say, that can be bottled in advance. A more tangy/fruity sour or punch. And a lower-strength spritz or highball that can be knocked up quickly or served from a jug (**see** *The Spritz – p.146* and *The Highball – p.128*).

Cut down on time spent waitressing by offering a few drinks that are a bit more DIY. Fill a big tureen with ice and a selection of homemade bottled cocktails and set it out on a table along with a selection of garnishes and

bitters, so guests can help themselves. Or break the ice with a beautiful punch that they can serve each other. If guests are feeling shy, they appreciate having something to do.

The febrile atmosphere of a party can make people very thirsty. So longer, lighter drinks like spritzes and highballs are often a sensible move. Consider serving cocktails that are usually served up, on ice – Manhattans, Margaritas and Aviations are all great on the rocks. Punches and cups, which get weaker the longer they sit on ice, are good long-distance drinks, too.

There's always a time in the night, I find, when suddenly everyone craves an ice-cold beer – so I keep a stash of well-chilled Sols or Coronas for when that moment strikes.

Everyone, whether they drink alcohol or not, will also appreciate some good booze-free options. And the choice of non-alcoholic drinks is better than ever these days. Tangy kombucha, alcohol-free beer, sparkling jasmine tea or Lyre's Campari-like bitter with tonic are all good for scratching the itch. Make sure there are jugs of iced water, garnished with cucumber, lemon or mint, freely available too.

And in the midst of all your planning, don't forget about food. It will help to keep everyone's energy up and make the drinks taste twice as good.

TO DO THE NIGHT BEFORE

- Make any syrups or sherbets so they have time to cool down and/or infuse. Bottle/seal in a container.

- Pre-batch any alcoholic components, e.g. spirits, vermouths, bitters. Bottle and put in the fridge to chill.

- Chill any mixers, sparkling wine, soda etc.

- Prepare ice blocks/fill ice trays/lay in bags of ice.

TO DO DURING THE DAY

- Squeeze any citrus fruits and put juice in the fridge to chill.

- Pre-batch any remaining ingredients – except fizzy ones – and chill.

- Make tea, if required, and leave to cool.

- Make a practice cocktail – adjust if necessary.

- Lay out glasses on a big tray and/or punch bowl and ladle.

- Slice/pick any garnishes and store in the fridge in some Tupperware lined with damp kitchen roll.

TO DO 15 MINUTES BEFORE

- Do the final mixing of any punches, garnish and add ice.

- Ready a few glasses with ice and a garnish.

TO DO 10 MINUTES BEFORE

- Prepare a few finished drinks so they're ready for the first guests.

- Fill a few more glasses with ice and garnishes so they are ready to go.

TO DO 5 MINUTES BEFORE

- Sit down and have a drink yourself.

THE TEN COCKTAIL COMMANDMENTS

---

1. A GOOD GLASS IS A COLD GLASS: ALWAYS FREEZE OR CHILL YOUR GLASSWARE

2. MEASURE INGREDIENTS ACCURATELY (AT LEAST UNTIL YOU'VE FAMILIARISED YOURSELF WITH THE RECIPE)

3. ENSURE LEMON AND LIME JUICE IS ALWAYS FRESHLY SQUEEZED

4. KEEP MIXERS AND SPARKLING WINES FIZZY AND WELL CHILLED

5. IF IN DOUBT, USE MORE ICE – ALLOW AT LEAST FIVE CUBES PER DRINK

6. SHAKE REALLY HARD; STIR STEADILY AND SLOWLY

7. TASTE AND ADJUST, IF NECESSARY – AND ALWAYS HAVE A LITTLE EXTRA OF YOUR INGREDIENTS ON HAND IN CASE YOU NEED TO TWEAK

8. PRESENTATION IS IMPORTANT – DON'T SKIP THE GARNISH

9. IT'S BETTER TO DO A SIMPLE RECIPE BRILLIANTLY THAN A COMPLICATED ONE POORLY

10. NEVER PUT THE ICE TRAY BACK IN THE FREEZER WITHOUT REFILLING IT FIRST

RECIPES

THE GIN SOUR

GLASS: *cocktail glass*

GARNISH: *lemon or orange twist*

METHOD: *shake and strain*

50ml gin

25ml lemon juice

12.5ml sugar syrup

If you only commit one recipe to memory, make it the 4:2:1 sour – because four parts strong, two parts sour, one part sweet recurs time and again in the cocktail canon.

It's the formula for the Daiquiri, the Whiskey Sour, the Bramble and the Basil Smash, and the backbone of the Mojito, Collins and French 75. With a bit of a tweak to allow for less-sweet liqueurs, it also informs the Aviation and the Margarita. Pick apart many punches, and you'll find a 4:2:1 sour at their core. Once you know it, you'll spot it everywhere in a multitude of forms.

You can make a 4:2:1 sour out of any white spirit. But it's the Gin Sour that I find the most useful; it's key to so many classics and can be adapted in many ways.

You can lengthen it with sparkling wine or soda or jasmine tea to make a refreshing punch. Or sweeten it with a homemade flavoured syrup, instead of plain syrup, or maraschino or triple sec (if you're using liqueurs instead of 2:1 sugar syrup, just add an extra teaspoon or two).

You can shake it with cucumber, or basil, or lavender or mint. Or serve it over ice and drizzle it with blackberry liqueur or Campari. You can spike it with orange bitters or scent it with a spritz of absinthe. It's happy on the rocks, in a coupe, or blitzed with ice in a blender. It can be shaken or mixed in a jug.

If you take away the alcohol and add water – hey presto, you've got lemonade. And if you don't have lemons, no matter – it works equally well with lime.

Once you know the 4:2:1 formula, you can busk a drink out of just about anything: the dregs of a party, corner-shop booze or the finest gin and lemons from Amalfi. Consider it your cocktail survival kit.

FRENCH 75

Delve into the history books and you'll find French 75s made with apple brandy, gin and grenadine, served with sparkling wine and without. In New Orleans, the French 75 is traditionally made with cognac. This gin-based version of French 75, though, is the one that I like best. A fantastic party drink that hits, in the words of *The Savoy Cocktail Book*, 'with remarkable precision'.

GLASS: *cocktail glass*

GARNISH: *lemon twist*

METHOD: *shake the gin, lemon juice and sugar syrup, strain into the glass, top with sparkling wine and stir*

25ml gin
12.5ml lemon juice
7.25ml sugar syrup
50ml sparkling wine

AVIATION

This sherbetty classic from the early 1900s is the perfect marriage of prettiness and power. Some versions also add a dash of crème de violette but I think the maraschino's subtle floral note is enough. If you add a dash of orange bitters, it's called a Casino. Also good shaken with a few lavender heads or a sprig of lemon verbena.

GLASS: *cocktail glass*

GARNISH: *lemon twist and/or maraschino cherry*

METHOD: *shake and strain*

50ml gin
20ml lemon juice
15ml Luxardo Maraschino Liqueur

BASIL SMASH

Basil is wonderful with gin – and nowhere is it better than in this box-fresh
smash by Joerg Meyer, the ebullient bartender/owner of Le Lion in Hamburg.
Meyer recommends including the basil stems as well as the leaves in the drink,
to really maximise the grassy, clove-spiked scent. Le Lion regulars like it with
75ml of gin, instead of 50ml – but I'll leave that up to you.

GLASS: *rocks*

GARNISH: *basil sprig*

METHOD: *roughly tear up the basil
leaves (including stalks) and chuck in
the shaker with the other ingredients.
Shake and strain into a glass full to
the brim with cracked ice.*

50ml gin

25ml lemon juice

12.5ml sugar syrup

Big handful of basil
leaves

BRAMBLE

This '80s classic is a brilliant example of how easily the 4:2:1 sour can be tweaked to create a whole new drink. If you don't have crème de mûre, it also works with cassis or Campari. Based on a recipe by Dick Bradsell, one of the godfathers of modern bartending.

GLASS: *rocks*

GARNISH: *lemon slice*

METHOD: *shake the first three ingredients with ice and strain into a glass filled with crushed ice. Drizzle the blackberry liqueur over the top so it bleeds into the drink.*

50ml gin
25ml lemon juice
10ml sugar syrup
10ml blackberry liqueur
　　　(crème de mûre)

BRAMBLE

SENCHA TEA COLLINS

An infusion of grassy sencha tea gives this Collins a subtle hint of umami – a sophisticated, refreshing drink perfect for summer. Adapted from a recipe in *Batched & Bottled* by Max and Noel Venning.

GLASS: *rocks or highball*

GARNISH: *lemon twist*

METHOD: *shake the gin, lemon juice and sugar syrup and strain over ice. Top with soda water and stir.*

50ml sencha tea-infused gin*

25ml lemon juice

12.5ml sugar syrup

75ml soda water

*The original recipe calls for a syrup made from hot sencha tea, but I prefer cold-infusing the tea into the gin as it's quicker and gives a more delicate taste. To make 50ml of sencha tea gin, combine 1 tsp of sencha tea with 50ml of gin in a little jug and leave to infuse for 30 minutes. Strain.

CORPSE REVIVER NO.2

In the early 1800s, cocktails were often taken as morning drinks and there were whole families of matutinal recipes: corpse revivers, eye-openers, fog-cutters, phlegm drivers. This recipe from *The Savoy Cocktail Book* of 1930 pays homage to that tradition with a splash of eye-opening absinthe. If you love the 4:2:1 Gin Sour, this is where you should head next.

GLASS: *cocktail glass*

GARNISH: *lemon twist*

METHOD: *shake and strain*

25ml gin

25ml lemon juice

25ml triple sec

25ml Cocchi Americano

2.5ml absinthe

THE MARTINI

GLASS: *cocktail glass*

GARNISH: *twist and/or olive*

METHOD: *stir and strain*

50ml gin
10ml dry vermouth
1 dash orange bitters (optional)

You could make a thousand Martinis and never make the same one twice. And that's why, I think, this incremental drink so endlessly fascinates.

Every now and again someone claims to have cracked the ultimate Martini formula; that it's 7:1 or 15:1 or even 3.7:1 (yes, really). But in my mind, making a Martini is less like composing a vaccine and more like cutting a diamond – each tiny decision you take makes it sparkle in a different way.

Modern-day Martinis tend to be on the dry side: 5 parts gin to 1 part vermouth, or thereabouts. Early incarnations of the cocktail, though, were often much wetter than that: two parts gin to one part vermouth, or even just 50/50. Doing it this way gives you a softer, fresher, aperitif-style drink.

If you flip the formula on its head, it's a Reverse Martini – a trick that also works with the Manhattan (a cocktail that, you may have noticed, has the same formula of spirit, vermouth and bitters as the Martini, just in a darker form). If you've got dry and white vermouth, a Martini is also good with a 50/50 mix of the two.

Pre-Prohibition Martinis were made with a dash of orange bitters – an aromatic touch I love. When it comes to the garnish I find it hard to choose between an olive and a lemon twist – so often, I'll have both.

I'm strongly of the view that a Martini should be stirred, rather than shaken. You want it poised, dense and silky, rather than perturbed.

Having said that, just occasionally, a Martini is good messy – thrown together by eye and served on the rocks. A different drink, but no less delicious. A diamond in the rough.

GIBSON ON THE ROCKS

The idea of serving a Martini on the rocks may shock some purists – but in the 1950s and '60s it was quite fashionable. The inclusion of pickled onions, of course, is what makes it a Gibson. Ernest Hemingway reputedly liked to garnish his Martinis with silverskins straight from the freezer.

GLASS: *rocks*

GARNISH: *three silverskin pickled onions*

METHOD: *stir and serve over ice*

50ml gin

10ml dry vermouth

5–10ml pickling vinegar from a jar of silverskin pickled onions (optional)

VESPER MARTINI

Shaking, rather than stirring, is positively encouraged with this Martini twist, which was created by Ian Fleming for the 1953 James Bond caper *Casino Royale*. Fleming's original recipe could floor a rhino – I've toned down the quantities a bit. It also called for Kina Lillet, a wine-based quinine aperitif that is now extinct. Cocchi Americano, though, is a fine substitute.

GLASS: *cocktail glass*

GARNISH: *lemon twist*

METHOD: *shake and strain*

45ml gin

15ml vodka

10ml Cocchi Americano

MARTINEZ

Can't decide whether to have a Martini or a Manhattan tonight? Then have a Martinez! Widely regarded as the precursor to the Martini, this Martini/Manhattan hybrid was originally made with either genever or Old Tom gin, two juniper spirits with a more full-bodied, sweeter style (and often a bit of cask character, too). In this version, maraschino liqueur steps in to provide some sweetness and body and the Angostura adds woody spice. Extremely sophisticated.

GLASS: *cocktail glass*

GARNISH: *orange twist*

METHOD: *stir and strain*

40ml dry gin

25ml red vermouth

5ml Luxardo Maraschino Liqueur

1 dash Angostura Bitters

JASMINE TEA MARTINI

My husband and I made this Martini for a house party once and served it from ice-packed tea pots, in tiny tea cups. It's a recipe that works with gin or vodka – I rather like the purity of vodka for this particular drink. White vermouth accentuates the jasmine's floral notes; dry vermouth draws out more of the aromatic green tea.

GLASS: *cocktail glass or little tea cup*

GARNISH: *lemon twist*

METHOD: *stir and strain*

50ml jasmine tea-infused gin or vodka*

10ml dry or white vermouth

*Infuse five jasmine tea pearls in 50ml of gin or vodka for 15 minutes. Strain.

JASMINE TEA MARTINI

NORDIC MARTINI

Aquavit's glacial notes of dill, caraway and fennel combine beautifully with juniper to create a Martini that's as cool and fresh as a snow-capped mountain. When it comes to the garnish, go on a raid of the Nordic larder. Herbs, pickles, even a rollmop herring could work. Or sip with some gravadlax on the side.

GLASS: *cocktail glass*

GARNISH: *lemon twist (discarded) and either pickles, dill or a cucumber ribbon on a cocktail stick*

METHOD: *stir and strain*

40ml gin

20ml aquavit

10ml dry vermouth

SMOKY MARTINI

Half a teaspoon of peated single malt is all it takes to give this Martini a savoury, smoky accent. Depending on your taste, and the whisky you use, you may find you want a little more. I like it with Lagavulin 16yo, an Islay malt with a billowing, sweet smokiness like lapsang souchong tea.

GLASS: *cocktail glass*

GARNISH: *orange twist*

METHOD: *stir and strain*

50ml gin

10ml dry vermouth

2.5ml peated Scotch whisky (I use Lagavulin 16yo)

THE OLD FASHIONED

GLASS: *rocks*

GARNISH: *lemon or orange twist*

METHOD: *stir with ice*

50ml bourbon/rye whiskey
5ml sugar syrup
1 dash bitters

Despite what the name might suggest, the Old Fashioned was not the world's first cocktail – drinks like the Sazerac (**see** – *p.96*) got there several decades before. But of all the bittered whiskey cocktails to emerge from America in the 1800s, it remains the best known and the most widely adored.

Part of its charm is its lack of pretentiousness – it can be made any time, any place, anywhere. It doesn't require fancy tools or, save the twist, fresh ingredients. It's an end-of-days kind of a drink.

The earliest Old Fashioneds were almost certainly made with rye whiskey. Sweet, nutty and spicy, rye gives the drink an almost tactile quality. I love Sazerac Rye and Rittenhouse with its notes of leather and cherrywood smoke. Bourbon gives you a drink that's a bit more mellow and rounded – Buffalo Trace, Woodford Reserve or the smooth-sipping wheated bourbon Maker's Mark would all be good. For other whiskey suggestions, **see** *The 12-Bottle Bar – p.15.*

A good selection of cocktail bitters will increase the mileage you can get out of this drink. Anything spicy, citrusy, nutty or chocolatey is almost certain to work.

At the height of its popularity, in the 1880s, the Old Fashioned wasn't just one drink, it was a whole genre: Americans drank Old Fashioneds made with rye, sweet gin, genever and imported French brandy. And that spirit-sugar-bitters formula can be adapted to suit all kinds of hard liquor. Over the page, you'll find a delicious Old Fashioned made with rum.

The Old Fashioned has a reputation for taking ages to make – a hangover, perhaps, from the days when it was sweetened with loaf sugar and required masses of stirring. If you use sugar syrup, however, it's the work of a moment. Either way, its enjoyment should not be rushed.

MAPLE & BACON OLD FASHIONED

Maple syrup gives depth and richness to this Old Fashioned; the salt makes it really moreish. Make double rounds of bacon as it will be gone in five seconds flat.

GLASS: *rocks*

GARNISH: *crisp shard of streaky bacon*

METHOD: *stir with ice*

50ml bourbon/rye whiskey

12.5ml maple syrup

Few flakes of salt (smoked salt is good too)

1 dash Angostura Bitters

SAZERAC

Derived from an elixir created by Antoine Peychaud at his apothecary in the French Quarter of New Orleans, this aromatic classic from the mid-1800s is a drink with a real aura. Early iterations were brandy-based, but now it's more often made with rye – some, in a nod to history, make it with a mix of the two. One of my favourite cocktails.

GLASS: *rocks*

GARNISH: *lemon twist*

METHOD: *traditionally the Sazerac is stirred and then served in a glass without ice as if it were some kind of medicine (which it sort of is). But I also like it on the rocks. Up to you.*

50ml bourbon/rye whiskey or cognac or a mix of the two

5ml sugar syrup

2.5ml absinthe

1 dash Angostura Bitters

2 dashes Peychaud's Bitters

FIG-LEAF OLD FASHIONED

One evening last summer, I was working in my study when the scent of sun-warmed fig leaves came drifting in through the window. I sat there inhaling its fruity/leafy/coconutty perfume and wondered if it might work with whiskey. I went outside, picked some leaves and this was the result. Good in a Rum Old Fashioned, too.

GLASS: *rocks*

GARNISH: *baby fig leaf/fig slice/ lemon or orange twist*

METHOD: *combine the whiskey and sugar syrup in a mixing glass, add the torn-up fig leaf and leave to infuse for half an hour. Strain into an ice-filled rocks glass, add the bitters and stir as normal.*

50ml bourbon/rye whiskey

5ml sugar syrup

2 dashes orange bitters

1 hand-sized fig leaf, roughly torn

MINT JULEP

The Mint Julep is really just an Old Fashioned that's been freshened up a little. Born on the sun-baked racetracks of Kentucky, it's divine on a hot day. A frozen glass (or even better, julep tin) is essential to this drink – done right, it should be a real finger-stinger.

GLASS: *highball or rocks*

GARNISH: *mint sprig and a straw*

METHOD: *shake and strain over lots of cracked ice. Keep churning and adding ice until the glass is completely full.*

50ml bourbon/rye whiskey

10ml sugar syrup

1 dash Angostura Bitters

6 mint leaves

RUM OLD FASHIONED

Rum's natural sweetness lends itself very well to an Old Fashioned – with more unctuous rums you may find you don't need any sugar syrup at all. Good as an after-dinner drink, with a piece of bitter black chocolate on the side.

GLASS: *rocks*

GARNISH: *orange twist*

METHOD: *stir with ice*

50ml dark rum

5ml sugar syrup

2 dashes orange, chocolate or walnut bitters

MONTE CARLO

A sweet-and-spicy whiskey drink halfway between a Sazerac and an Old Fashioned. In his 1948 *The Fine Art of Mixing Drinks*, writer David Embury makes an argument for shaking it, but I much prefer it stirred.

GLASS: *rocks*

GARNISH: *lemon twist*

METHOD: *stir with ice*

50ml bourbon/rye whiskey

10ml Bénédictine DOM

1 dash Angostura Bitters

THE DAIQUIRI

GLASS: *cocktail glass*

GARNISH: *none*

METHOD: *shake and strain*

50ml light/white rum
25ml lime juice
12.5ml sugar syrup

The Daiquiri has a bit of a corny reputation. But in its purest form, it's rather a subtle drink; an opalescent balancing act between sweet, sour and strong.

The Daiquiri was invented in Cuba, the country that gave the world dry white rum. And it's with a light Cuban rum such as Havana Club 3yo that it tastes its best. The rum's grassy, sugar-cane sweetness is there, along with a hint of vanilla. But the drink also reveals a side to this spirit that is a bit more unhinged: the ester-y, overripe fruit notes, like pineapple on the turn; the camphor and treacle and concrete; a whiff of peat smoke that could have drifted over from Islay.

When I think of the Daiquiri I think of coastlines and eye-dazzling blue seas, the crumbling glamour of Havana's charismatic bars: El Floridita, 'cradle of the Daiquiri', with its mahogany bar and red-tied barkeeps; the waterside La Terraza de Cojímar where Hemingway refuelled between fishing trips; cocktail hour, Sinatra-style, on the palm-fringed terrace of the grand old Hotel Nacional.

A Daiquiri, wherever you drink it, should be as refreshing as diving into a pool. Shake until the tin's so cold it hurts your hands.

Experiment with changing the sweetener; try demerara or honey syrup or elderflower cordial (for the latter you may need 5–10ml more). Substitute with maraschino liqueur or triple sec – or shock your guests with a round of Daiquiris spiked with cerulean blue curaçao.

Throw a few herbs in the shaker – mint, basil or lemon verbena all love rum. Or some tangy fresh fruit. A Daiquiri shaken with the flesh of a passion fruit is heaven on a stick.

BASIL & HONEY DAIQUIRI

This basil-flecked Daiquiri was one of the first cocktails I learned how to make and it remains one of my favourite twists. The honey adds a more rounded, golden sweetness than ordinary syrup. Based on a recipe by Daiquiri obsessive Simon Difford.

GLASS: *cocktail glass*

GARNISH: *basil sprig*

METHOD: *mix the honey and rum thoroughly in the base of the shaker. Add the other ingredients. Shake and strain.*

50ml light/white rum

25ml lime juice

15ml honey syrup (**see** *Sugar Syrups* – p.35)

6-8 basil leaves

DAIQUIRI ELIXIR

Just a teaspoon or two of Green Chartreuse turns up the dial on everything in the drink – the best way I can describe it is a Daiquiri in HD. No need for a garnish here – just close your eyes and drink it in. Based on a recipe by Simon Difford.

GLASS: *cocktail glass*

GARNISH: *none*

METHOD: *shake and strain*

50ml light/white rum

25ml lime juice

10ml sugar syrup

5-10ml Green Chartreuse

HEMINGWAY DAIQUIRI

Ernest Hemingway spent so much time propping up the bar at El Floridita
that the bartenders created a Daiquiri in his honour. The original, known as
the Papa Doble, contained heroic amounts of booze – this is a slightly adapted
version. Even so, it comes up quite big, so if you have a choice, go for a bigger
coupe. It's a beautiful, pale pink. Also good on the rocks.

GLASS: *cocktail glass*

GARNISH: *maraschino cherry and/or
grapefruit wedge*

METHOD: *shake and strain*

50ml light/white rum

25ml pink grapefruit juice

15ml lime juice

15ml Luxardo Maraschino Liqueur

FROZEN WATERMELON DAIQUIRI

The frozen watermelon chunks do the job of the ice here — and the result is cool pink perfection. You could add a few drops of rosewater, or swap the triple sec for maraschino liqueur too, if you like. A frozen Daiquiri that's the right side of tacky. (For more tips on making frozen drinks, **see** *Techniques – p.55.*)

GLASS: *cocktail glass*

GARNISH: *mint sprig*

METHOD: *blend hard and fast in a blender. Pour into glass.*

50ml light/white rum

30ml lime juice

15ml sugar syrup

10ml triple sec

1 large handful frozen, de-seeded watermelon chunks

FROZEN WATERMELON DAIQUIRI

PINEAPPLE & CARDAMOM DAIQUIRI

Cardamom's spicy, floral perfume is gorgeous but penetrating, so go easy on the muddling in this drink. You want it subtly scented, rather than soapy. If you can't get freshly juiced pineapple, just muddle in a handful of really ripe pineapple chunks instead.

GLASS: *cocktail glass*

GARNISH: *lime wheel*

METHOD: *muddle the cardamom pods very gently in the base of the shaker. Add the other ingredients, shake and strain.*

50ml light/white rum
20ml lime juice
20ml pineapple juice
2 cardamom pods
10ml sugar syrup
Hull of half a lime

PASSIONFRUIT DAIQUIRI

A starburst of deliciousness. Proof that simple is sometimes best.

GLASS: *cocktail glass*

GARNISH: *nothing*

METHOD: *shake and strain*

50ml light/white rum
25ml lime
12.5ml sugar syrup
Flesh of a passion fruit

THE NEGRONI

GLASS: *rocks*

GARNISH: *citrus twist, wedge or wheel*

METHOD: *stir with ice*

25ml gin
25ml red vermouth
25ml Campari

The ruby-red Negroni is a beautiful drink – and a wonderfully robust one, too. You can throw one together at high speed, and stir it with a finger, and it will still taste pretty good.

Bitter as medicine, and as syrupy-sweet; it's a taste both kind and cruel. It's a cocktail that makes your hair stand on end at the same time as it soothes.

The Negroni is part of the aperitivo family – a class of bitter-sweet, botanical drinks designed to prime the digestion for food. The word aperitivo derives from the Latin for 'to open', *aperire*.

It's a drink of anticipation, not just gastronomically, but socially too – if you're heading out for an evening of bar-hopping in Milan, there's nothing like a Negroni to put you in the mood.

I love a recipe that's equal-parts-everything. And especially one where you can substitute. I rarely negotiate on the Campari, but I'll often experiment with different gins and vermouths. One of my favourite sundowners is the Negroni Sbagliato (**see** – p.109) – or 'bungled Negroni' – which is made with prosecco instead of gin. A Negroni made with tequila or bourbon (**see** – p.108) is also nicer than you might think.

Embedded in the Negroni formula are two more simple but very fine drinks: the Milano Torino (equal parts Campari and vermouth) and the Gin & It (equal parts vermouth and gin). It's a cocktail that yields endless twists.

If you don't want a Negroni that knocks you sideways, be sure to stir with lots of ice. Serve in a handsome glass with a fragrant twist or a juicy orange slice.

WATERMELON NEGRONI

A deliciously summery twist on the Negroni created by Monica Berg, bartender/co-owner of Tayēr + Elementary in London. Strained, bottled and refrigerated, it will keep very well for a couple of days.

GLASS: *rocks*

GARNISH: *watermelon slice*

METHOD: *combine all the ingredients in a jug and leave to steep for two to three hours. Strain off the watermelon chunks, pour the Negroni over ice and stir as normal.*

25ml gin

25ml red vermouth

25ml Campari

One large handful de-seeded watermelon chunks

BOULEVARDIER

The brooding, whiskey-based cousin of the Negroni. If you like it with a bit more muscle, up the quantity of whiskey. Or try a dash of Angostura or orange bitters in the mix.

GLASS: *rocks*

GARNISH: *orange twist*

METHOD: *stir with ice*

25ml bourbon/rye whiskey

25ml red vermouth

25ml Campari

NEGRONI SBAGLIATO

Literally a 'bungled Negroni', the Negroni Sbagliato was supposedly invented at Bar Basso in Milan when a bartender making a Negroni accidentally reached for the prosecco instead of the gin. A spritz-y twist on the classic Negroni that lends itself to being mixed by the jugful for parties – or being served, as it is at Bar Basso, in foot-high, ice-filled goblets.

GLASS: *rocks*

GARNISH: *orange wheel*

METHOD: *build over ice*

25ml gin

25ml red vermouth

75ml sparkling wine

WHITE NEGRONI

If you like the taste of Campari, the French gentian liqueur Suze will almost certainly be up your street. It has less of the smoky-sweet/rhubarb notes, and more parched herbs and citrus peel. But its texture and bittersweetness are of the same intensity. A fun substitute for Campari, not just for the taste, but for the golden colour, too.

GLASS: *rocks*

GARNISH: *grapefruit twist*

METHOD: *stir on ice*

25ml gin
25ml Suze
25ml Cocchi Americano

COFFEE NEGRONI

Just when you thought the Negroni couldn't get any more bitter, or better, along comes a twist with coffee liqueur. A really A-grade liqueur is key here, so you feel the full force of the coffee's darker, roasty notes – I use Mr Black. A Negroni variation that would be equally good as an aperitivo or a digestif.

GLASS: *rocks*

GARNISH: *orange twist*

METHOD: *stir on ice*

25ml gin
25ml red vermouth
25ml Campari
10ml coffee liqueur

FROZEN ORANGE NEGRONI

A Negroni lengthened with orange juice (or grapefruit juice) is good
– a Negroni blitzed with orange juice and ice is even better. A thirst-quenching twist on the classic aperitivo by American bartender and drinks writer Jeffrey Morgenthaler.

GLASS: *rocks*

GARNISH: *orange wedge or twist*

METHOD: *blitz with six ice cubes and pour into the glass*

30ml gin
30ml red vermouth
30ml Campari
20ml sugar syrup
1 dash orange bitters (optional)
Juice of an orange

THE MANHATTAN

GLASS: *cocktail glass*

GARNISH: *orange or lemon twist and maraschino cherries*

METHOD: *stir and strain*

50ml bourbon/rye whiskey

25ml red vermouth

1 dash Angostura Bitters

5ml syrup from a jar of Luxardo maraschino cherries (optional)

No one knows for sure where or when the Manhattan was created – but by the time the 1880s rolled round, it was one of the hottest bar-calls in New York.

Back then, it was often embellished with a dash of absinthe or orange curaçao, and a little maraschino liqueur. It's a simpler cocktail these days, but no less glamorous.

There are three main types of Manhattan: Dry (made exclusively with dry vermouth), Perfect (made with a 50/50 mix of red and dry vermouth) and Sweet (made with red vermouth and a spoonful of maraschino cherry syrup).

A Dry Manhattan is so rasping it's pretty much undrinkable in my view. But a Manhattan on the sweet side is really quite sublime.

The reason you need all that sweetness is to balance the bitterness – because all three ingredients in this drink have a lot of astringent, woody spice. If you're serving your Manhattan on the rocks – which is another nice way to have it – you'll almost certainly need that extra bump of sugar, too.

Modern Manhattans are usually seasoned with Angostura Bitters, but back in the late 19th century orange bitters were more widely used. Walnut bitters, chocolate bitters, grapefruit bitters, even a dash of minty Peychaud's would all bring something interesting to this drink.

Half the fun of a Manhattan, of course, is the whiskey-soaked cocktail cherry at the end. So don't stint on the garnish – put two or three cherries in.

REVERSE MANHATTAN

For a lighter take on the Manhattan, you can simply flip the formula (a hack that also works very well with a dry Martini). I don't think it needs the sugar syrup when it's this way round – once you've upped the vermouth, the cocktail is sweet enough. Aromatic and spicy – a lovely pre-prandial drink.

GLASS: *cocktail glass*

GARNISH: *orange twist*

METHOD: *stir and strain*

25ml bourbon/rye whiskey

50ml red vermouth

1 dash Angostura Bitters

VIEUX CARRÉ

This complicated mash-up between a Manhattan and a Sazerac was born in the New Orleans French Quarter some time in the 1930s. Its name, which translates literally as 'old square', is what the French Quarter was called in Creole. A nod to the cocktail's medicinal roots that's complex and fortifying.

GLASS: *rocks*

GARNISH: *lemon twist*

METHOD: *stir on ice*

20ml bourbon/rye whiskey

20ml cognac

20ml red vermouth

10ml Bénédectine DOM

2 dashes Peychaud's Bitters

1 dash Angostura Bitters

WHITE MANHATTAN

As I've already said, I'm no fan of the Dry Manhattan – I find it rather abrasive. But this pale-gold twist on the Manhattan, which is made with sweet white vermouth rather than dry, is absolutely delicious. Subtle, sophisticated. And dry. But in the right way.

GLASS: *cocktail glass*

GARNISH: *grapefruit twist*

METHOD: *stir and strain*

50ml bourbon/rye whiskey

25ml white vermouth

2 dashes orange bitters

RUSTY MANHATTAN

This Manhattan twist is a tribute to the Rusty Nail – a whisky-based nightcap that we have a bit of a soft spot for in our house. Drambuie liqueur, which is made from a blend of Scotch, honey and botanicals, gives it a spicy, slightly aniseedy edge. A rich, warming cocktail that's best sipped after dinner, or on a winter's night.

GLASS: *rocks*

GARNISH: *lemon twist*

METHOD: *stir and strain over ice*

35ml bourbon, rye whiskey or Scotch whisky

15ml Drambuie

25ml red vermouth

1 dash orange bitters

RUSTY MANHATTAN

ROB ROY

A Rob Roy is essentially just a Manhattan made with Scotch whisky instead of American whiskey – where it gets interesting is when you use a Scotch whisky that's slightly peaty. A really big-hitting Islay malt such as Laphroaig might be a bit much, but a gently smoky blend like Johnnie Walker Black Label works very well.

GLASS: *cocktail glass*

GARNISH: *orange twist and a cherry*

METHOD: *stir and strain*

50ml Scotch whisky

25ml red vermouth

5ml syrup from a jar of Luxardo maraschino cherries (optional)

1 dash Angostura Bitters

MANHATTAN 1890ˢ-STYLE

This recipe is taken from *The Flowing Bowl* by William Schmidt, published in 1891. Intense, aromatic, complex and unadorned, this is one for serious Manhattan devotees.

GLASS: *cocktail glass*

GARNISH: *none*

METHOD: *stir and strain*

50ml rye whiskey

25ml red vermouth

2.5ml sugar syrup

2 dashes orange bitters

5 drops absinthe

THE MARGARITA

GLASS: *rocks or cocktail glass*

GARNISH: *salt rim and optional lime wedge*

METHOD: *shake, strain and either serve up or on the rocks*

50ml tequila
25ml triple sec
20ml lime juice

There's always an evening in early summer when the light is golden and the air smells different and I suddenly find myself craving a Margarita. I don't know if it's the promise of salt, or citrus, or that just-rained-on-sidewalks thing you get in all the best agave spirits, but it makes me stop whatever I'm doing and head straight into the kitchen in search of my lime squeezer.

Of course, the problem with crave-y drinks like this is that it's impossible to have just one. So perhaps the first rule of making Margaritas should be: always make double the amount.

The next rule, if you want to pace yourself, is always serve them on ice. Margaritas tend to taste more refreshing that way. And they go a bit further, too.

The Margarita is cool because it ventures to places where other cocktails fear to tread. It can do smoky and spicy and savoury – it's salty in the truest sense.

The Margarita recipe we start this chapter with is a classic formula – but like a lot of tequila fans, I think I actually prefer the Tommy's Margarita overleaf. Using agave syrup instead of triple sec, as the Tommy's does, produces a drink that's just a little bit more harmonious. And there's something nice about having two expressions of the agave plant in one glass.

A Margarita isn't a Margarita without a glittering rim of salt. You'll find tips on how to do a salt rim – and spicy variations – in The Garnish chapter of this book (**see** – *p.66*). If you want to give people the choice of with-or-without, just go halfway round the rim. Or if time is short, or the craving too great, just sprinkle a few salt flakes straight in.

TOMMY'S MARGARITA

This variation on the classic Margarita tends to be the one favoured by agave aficionados. Created in the 1980s at the San Fran tequila bar Tommy's, it doubles down on agave – the succulent that tequila is made from – by using sweet agave syrup instead of triple sec. And it's always served on the rocks. Also good with a more flinty, smoky mezcal.

GLASS: *rocks*

GARNISH: *salt rim and lime wedge*

METHOD: *shake and strain over ice*

50ml tequila

25ml lime juice

12.5ml agave syrup

2 dashes orange bitters

CHAMPAGNE MARGARITA

I can't think of a combination more hedonistic than tequila and champagne – and this one is wickedly good. It would be a great drink to kick off a party, or even as a thirst-quenching punch – just lengthen with a bit of sparkling or still water and charge with lots of ice. For more elegance, serve in a coupe, undiluted, over a single ice cube.

GLASS: *cocktail glass or rocks*

GARNISH: *lime wheel*

METHOD: *shake the first three ingredients and strain over ice and top with sparkling wine*

50ml tequila

25ml lime juice

12.5ml sugar syrup

50ml sparkling wine

HIBISCUS MARGARITA

This garnet-coloured cocktail takes its inspiration from the Mexican drink agua fresca, a thirst-quenching non-alcoholic cooler made from hibiscus flowers. Hibiscus has a tart, cranberry-like taste that goes brilliantly with tequila and lime. A refreshing take on the Margarita that would be good for a barbecue.

GLASS: *rocks*

GARNISH: *lime and orange slices*

METHOD: *no need to shake this one – just mix in a jug and pour over ice*

50ml tequila

25ml lime juice

15ml sugar syrup

35ml hibiscus water*

2 dashes orange bitters

Few flakes of salt

*Dried hibiscus flowers are easy to find online or in any shop that has a reasonable selection of herbs and spices. Combine one large handful of dried hibiscus flowers in boiling water and leave to infuse until cool. Strain and bottle.

PINEAPPLE & SHICHIMI MARGARITA

Tropical tang meets Japanese fire in this Margarita twist by Sydney's Cantina OK! Bar. It's best with freshly juiced pineapple but if you can't get hold of the fresh stuff, use a dash of packaged juice plus some muddled cubes of fresh pineapple. Shichimi adds a spicy kick and a pop of vibrant colour, too.

GLASS: *cocktail glass*

GARNISH: *rim of salt and shichimi*

METHOD: *shake and strain*

45ml tequila

20ml lime juice

20ml pineapple juice (freshly juiced, if possible)

10ml agave syrup

PINEAPPLE & SHICHIMI MARGARITA

MEXICAN JUMPING BEAN

Not really a Margarita, granted, but if you've got what you need to make a Tommy's then you're already two-thirds of the way there. It's important to shake the coffee while it's really hot, to get the creamy head on the drink. And shake with even more ice than usual, so it cools fast without getting too dilute. A class-A recipe by journalist and cocktailian Richard Godwin that is (whisper it) possibly even better than the Espresso Martini.

GLASS: *cocktail glass*

GARNISH: *3 coffee beans floated on top*

METHOD: *while the coffee is still piping hot, mix it and the syrup in the shaker, add the tequila and shake with lots of ice. Strain.*

50ml tequila

30ml really strong, really hot coffee

10ml agave syrup (or sugar syrup, in which case up it to 15ml)

PINK GRAPEFRUIT & CHILLI MARGARITA

Sweet, sour, salt, heat – this cocktail gets all the synapses firing. Play around with the garnish to give it different accents – even coriander might be nice. Dial the chilli up or down according to your taste.

GLASS: *rocks*

GARNISH: *lime wedge or mint sprig (or a red chilli if you're brave)*

METHOD: *give the chilli a gentle muddle in the bottom of the shaker with the tequila. Add the other ingredients, shake and strain over ice.*

50ml tequila

12.5ml lime juice

12.5ml sugar syrup

50ml pink grapefruit juice

5 thin slices of chilli

Few flakes of salt

THE SPRITZ

GLASS: *rocks or large wine glass*

GARNISH: *orange or lemon slice and a green olive*

METHOD: *build over ice*

75ml sparkling wine

50ml Campari, Aperol or other bitter aperitif

25ml soda water

There are many variations on the spritz – what unites them all is the sparkle. That little explosion of bubbles that gives the drink, and the spirits, a lift.

The original spritz was the white wine spritzer – known in the 19th century as the hock and soda. In a poem, Lord Byron declared this combination of sweet German white wine and soda to be his number one hangover cure.

With the arrival of Campari in the 1860s, the spritz took a bittersweet turn. Bartenders added prosecco and ice. And by the late 20th century, the modern-day spritz al bitter was born.

The word 'spritz' comes from the German word *spritzen*, which means 'to spray'. But it's northern Italy that remains the heartland of spritz drinking today. On a summer evening in Milan or Venice, it's clinking spritzes on all sides – bright orange Aperol for the Venetians, and red Campari for the Milanese.

The spritz suits spontaneity. I don't think I've ever seen an Italian measure one out. But the 3-2-1 formula – 3 parts prosecco, 2 parts bitter aperitif, 1 part soda – is a good rule of thumb.

This formula is very forgiving and works with all kinds of bittered aperitifs: Suze, Cocchi Americano, Lillet, Cynar, every colour of vermouth. If you don't have any sparkling wine, just use still white wine and soda.

A spritz is at its most delicious with something salty to eat on the side; some crisps, salami or bruschetta, to whet the appetite. In Venice, spritzes are often served with a green olive actually *in* the drink – which may sound odd, but turns out to be a total masterstroke.

HUGO SPRITZ

Supposedly born in South Tyrol, the Hugo Spritz takes many forms – I've come across versions sweetened with lemon syrup, elderflower cordial, lemon balm syrup and elderflower liqueur. Elderflower cordial is a good place to start, though. Or elderflower liqueur for a bit more oomph. A Hugo Spritz with lemon verbena syrup and a squeeze of lemon would be very good, too.

GLASS: *rocks or large wine glass*

GARNISH: *mint sprig*

METHOD: *combine the first three ingredients in a glass with lots of ice (make sure the cordial/liqueur is well incorporated and not just sitting in a puddle at the bottom). Give the mint leaves a smack and stir through the drink, whole.*

100ml sparkling wine

12.5ml elderflower cordial (or liqueur)

25ml soda water

10 mint leaves

LIME & BASIL SPRITZ

The first time I had this spritz was in the grounds of Buckingham Palace – but that's a story for another time. Tart lime, fresh basil and vanilla-kissed white vermouth come together in a drink that's gloriously summery and light.

GLASS: *rocks or large wine glass*

GARNISH: *lime wheel*

METHOD: *build over ice*

75ml sparkling wine

50ml white vermouth

25ml soda water

Squeeze of lime

6 basil leaves

ROME WITH A VIEW

Dry vermouth adds a slightly more savoury dimension to the classic spritz in this tangy twist by Michael McIlroy of Attaboy, New York. You don't have to shake it, but it will be a better drink if you do.

GLASS: *rocks or highball*

GARNISH: *orange slice*

METHOD: *shake the first four ingredients and strain over ice. Top with soda and stir.*

25ml Campari

25ml dry vermouth

25ml lime juice

12.5ml sugar syrup

50ml soda water

YUZU & JASMINE SPRITZ

A delicate, low-alcohol spritz that marries sherbetty yuzu fruit with fragrant jasmine tea. I use Saicho Sparkling Jasmine Tea, which is lightly sweetened with grape juice. If you have a sparkling tea that's unsweetened – or a very tart yuzushu – you may want to add a dash of sugar syrup. A recipe that also works brilliantly with sparkling wine in place of jasmine tea.

GLASS: *rocks*

GARNISH: *cucumber and/or edible flower*

METHOD: *build over ice*

75ml yuzushu
50ml sparkling jasmine tea
5–10ml sugar syrup (optional)

ROSÉ SPRITZ

A beautiful, pale pink spritz that people will drink by the jugful. You could make it with sparkling rosé for more fizziness, but I like its subtle sparkle.

GLASS: *rocks*

GARNISH: *pink grapefruit wedge and cucumber wheel*

METHOD: *build over ice*

75ml dry rosé wine

50ml Cocchi Americano

25ml soda water

ARTICHOKE SPRITZ

The Italian artichoke amaro Cynar (pronounced cheee-nar) is strange and wonderful stuff. It has a bittersweetness like burnt sugar and smouldering, woody spice. It's a great sub in almost any drink where you'd use Campari or red vermouth: in a Negroni, say, or a Manhattan. It also makes a nice spritz that's more on the moody side.

GLASS: *rocks*

GARNISH: *orange slice*

METHOD: *build over ice*

60ml sparkling wine

60ml Cynar artichoke amaro

25ml soda water

THE GIMLET

GLASS: *cocktail glass*

GARNISH: *lime twist*

METHOD: *shake and strain*

50ml gin
12.5ml lime juice
12.5ml sugar syrup
Hull of half a lime

The original Gimlet wasn't really a cocktail – it was an alcoholic vehicle for vitamin C. Devised by naval officers in the early 1900s to ward off scurvy, it was often just a robust equal parts Rose's Lime Cordial and gin.

I salute those who stay true to that recipe, but I find it rather sickly. I much prefer a Gimlet made with gin, sugar syrup and a jolt of fresh lime. I stole the idea of throwing a lime peel in the shaker from Tom Macy of the Clover Club in Brooklyn – it's a great way to add a little extra citric shock.

Intensity is key to a Gimlet – it should be noticeably more concentrated, and less juicy, than a classic 4:2:1 sour.

You can make a Gimlet with shop-bought cordial – Belvoir and Thorncroft (especially the nettle cordial) are two good brands. But if you use a homemade sugar syrup, you can flavour it yourself – and that's where the Gimlet gets really fun.

First thing in the morning, have a riffle through your window box or garden and see if there's a herb or flower that smells especially nice. Pick a handful (only edible varieties, obviously), cover with 100ml of 2:1 sugar syrup and leave to infuse until six o'clock – and then make a Gimlet with the result. I've made Gimlets flavoured with fig leaves, lemon thyme, scented geranium leaves, even honeysuckle blooms with this technique – for more tips on flavouring and infusing, **see** *Sugar Syrups – p.32.*

Tart fruit syrups are great in a Gimlet: gooseberry, rhubarb or pink grapefruit. Or play up to its glacial side with more green and vegetal flavours – a Gimlet shaken with a few basil or lovage leaves, or some cubes of peeled cucumber, is wonderfully fresh and crunchy.

GRAPEFRUIT GIMLET

This pearlescent Gimlet is a hymn to grapefruit in all its forms: the marmalade-y peel, the sun-kissed juiciness and the zesty perfume. A taut, tart, complex drink – what the Gimlet is all about.

GLASS: *cocktail glass*

GARNISH: *grapefruit twist*

METHOD: *shake and strain*

50ml gin

10ml lime juice

5ml pink grapefruit juice

12.5ml grapefruit syrup (**see** *Sugar Syrups – p.33*)

FLAMINGO GIMLET

Cherry-red Peychaud's Bitters layer up the Gimlet with subtle notes of caraway, cinnamon and spearmint – and a pretty pink colour, too. Invented by me, and christened by Declan McGurk, former boss of bars at The Savoy.

GLASS: *cocktail glass*

GARNISH: *lime twist*

METHOD: *shake and strain*

50ml gin

12.5ml lime juice

12.5ml sugar syrup

4 dashes Peychaud's Bitters (or other red Creole-style bitters)

Hull of half a lime

TARRAGON GIMLET

Grassy, anise-y and pure, almost sorbet-like in its refreshingness, this is a stunning drink. I rather like it over ice, but it works with or without. When it comes to making the syrup infusion, really pack the tarragon in. You cannot use too much. Adapted from a recipe in *Herb* by Mark Diacono, a great field guide to cooking and drinking herbs of all kinds.

GLASS: *rocks or cocktail glass*

GARNISH: *tarragon sprig*

METHOD: *shake and serve up or over ice*

50ml gin

12.5ml lime juice

12.5ml tarragon syrup (**see** *Sugar Syrups – p.32*)

Hull of half a lime

ROSEHIP GIMLET

The orange-red hips of the dog rose – a rambling variety that grows wild in hedgerows and lanes all over the UK – makes a beautiful pale-pink syrup that tastes like Turkish Delight. The best time for foraging is very late summer or early autumn.

GLASS: *cocktail glass*

GARNISH: *lemon or lime twist. A rosehip would be pretty, too.*

METHOD: *shake and strain*

50ml gin

12.5ml lime juice

12.5ml rosehip syrup (**see** *Sugar Syrups – p.33*)

Hull of half a lime

ROSEHIP GIMLET

TOMATO GIMLET

You could have a lot of fun experimenting with different varieties of tomato in this drink, which oscillates intriguingly between sweet and fruity and green/umami. The sugar may need adjusting by a few millilitres depending on the ripeness of the tomatoes you use.

GLASS: *cocktail glass*

GARNISH: *basil leaf*

METHOD: *muddle the cherry tomatoes in the bottom of the shaker. Add the other ingredients, shake and double strain.*

50ml gin

10ml sugar syrup

12.5ml lime juice

3 halved cherry tomatoes

Hull of half a lime

SILVER BULLET

Kümmel's piercing, caraway flavour can be pretty divisive – but if you like it, there are few better ways to enjoy it than in this potent classic from the 1920s. Not strictly a Gimlet, I realise, but a cocktail that behaves in much the same way.

GLASS: *cocktail glass*

GARNISH: *lemon twist*

METHOD: *shake and strain*

50ml gin

10ml lemon juice

10ml Kümmel

THE WHISKEY SOUR
(& OTHER BROWN SOURS)

GLASS: *rocks*

GARNISH: *lemon twist and cherry*

METHOD: *shake and strain over ice (preferably one large hunk)*

50ml bourbon/rye whiskey
25ml lemon juice
12.5ml sugar syrup
1 dash Angostura Bitters
15ml egg white

Whiskey. Lemon juice. Syrup. Bitters. Raw egg white. It's an ugly old recipe on paper. But something magic happens to these ingredients when you give them a really hard shake. All the pointy elbows and shrill top notes, the hot alcohols and jangly proteins soften and lengthen and harmonise, and create something utterly new – a pillowy, aromatic sunshine-yellow sour that hits you pleasantly in the solar plexus.

The Whiskey Sour is a drink that can take a lot of sweetness – I like it best with an easy-sipping bourbon. If you find it lacks definition, you can always add more bitters.

I always feel slightly horrified adding the egg white – but when I taste the end result, I'm always glad I did. It binds the drink and lifts it; gives it more generosity in the mouth. If it turns you off, though, leave it out (or use chickpea water – **see** *Non-Alcoholic Ingredients – p.26*).

A good Whiskey Sour is shout-out-loud amazing – but a bad one is a real car crash. So this is one recipe where I would strongly recommend sticking rigidly to the rules. Use eggs and lemons that are as fresh as possible. Shake with lots of ice and shake extra hard, so it really fluffs up. And serve over one slow-melting ice block so it doesn't dilute too fast.

The garnish is the part of the Whiskey Sour where you can have real fun. Scent the surface with a fragrant orange twist or a spritz of rosewater. Dropper little dots of Angostura Bitters on the top and drag a toothpick through them to create patterns, barista-style. Or just lazily spoon one cherry into the drink, so the scarlet syrup drizzles through the foam.

AMARETTO SOUR

I spent a lot of the late '90s drinking Amaretto Sours. And then spent the next 20 years giving them a wide berth. It was only recently, in a fit of nostalgia, that I decided to try this variation by Jeffrey Morganthaler and it blew me away.

GLASS: *rocks*

GARNISH: *lemon twist and a maraschino cherry*

METHOD: *shake and train over ice*

25ml bourbon/rye whiskey

45ml amaretto liqueur

30ml lemon juice

5ml sugar syrup

15ml egg white

PENICILLIN

The name alludes to the medicinal properties, but also taste, of this smoky Scotch cocktail – which is essentially an iced hot toddy. Be brave and try it with a full-on peaty malt like Talisker or Laphroaig – it's more easy-drinking than you might think. Or use a more subtly smoky blend such as Johnnie Walker Black. If you don't have ginger liqueur, you could also use ginger syrup (**see** *Sugar Syrups – p.33*). Adapted from the classic created by Sam Ross at Milk & Honey, New York in 2005.

GLASS: *rocks*

GARNISH: *lemon twist and/or fresh ginger slice*

METHOD: *shake and strain over ice*

50ml peaty Scotch whisky

15ml ginger liqueur

20ml lemon juice

20ml honey syrup (**see** *Sugar Syrups – p.35*)

NEW YORK SOUR

This is a real showstopper of a drink – the beautiful red wine bleeding into the sunshine yellow sour below. Flavour-wise it works best with a red wine that's on the fruity side – a cheap and cheerful merlot or a Beaujolais would be great. But just use whatever you have open.

GLASS: *rocks*

GARNISH: *lemon twist*

METHOD: *shake the first five ingredients with ice and strain over ice. Carefully pour the red wine over the top to create a crimson float.*

50ml bourbon/rye whiskey

25ml lemon juice

12.5ml sugar syrup

1 dash Angostura Bitters

15ml egg white

For the float: **30ml** red wine

AIR MAIL

You could call this a sparkling Rum Sour, a champagne cocktail with a bit more sass to it, or a Rum Punch with the lift of a spritz – either way it's a gorgeous combination of pungent, rum-soaked fruit, sharp lime and tongue-tingling fizz. A great party drink.

GLASS: *rocks*

GARNISH: *mint sprig*

METHOD: *shake the first three ingredients with ice. Strain over ice and top with sparkling wine. Stir.*

30ml golden/dark rum

10ml lime juice

15ml honey syrup (**see** *Sugar Syrups – p.35*)

50ml sparkling wine

APPLE & BAY LEAF SOUR

Buoyantly fruity apple brandy meets cool, eucalyptus-like bay in this autumnal sour twist. It would work with cognac, too, but you'd miss the apple hit.

GLASS: *rocks*

GARNISH: *bay leaf or orange twist*

METHOD: *shake and strain*

50ml Calvados apple brandy or applejack

25ml lemon juice

12.5ml bay leaf syrup (**see** *Sugar Syrups – p.33*)

2 dashes orange bitters

15ml egg white

SIDECAR

Sidecars often end up being too sweet or too sour. But this formula, I hope you'll agree, hits the spot. If you like this 1920s classic, you may also like my Stoned Sidecar: 50ml cognac, 12.5ml triple sec, 25ml lemon juice and 12.5ml Merlet peach or apricot liqueur.

GLASS: *cocktail glass*

GARNISH: *lemon twist*

METHOD: *shake and strain*

50ml cognac

25ml triple sec

15ml lemon juice

THE HIGHBALL

GLASS: *highball*

GARNISH: *citrus wedge*

METHOD: *build over ice*

50ml gin
120ml tonic water

At the heart of every drinking culture is a drink that is long and fizzy; an easy, crowd-pleasing riff on the fuel upon which that community runs.

In Andalusia it's the Rebujito: dry sherry and cold 7-Up. In Tokyo it's the Whisky Highball, served with a twist and hand-cut ice. At sundown in the Douro, they press a white port and tonic into your hand. It's the Paloma in Mexico, the Cuba Libre in the Caribbean and the Americano in Milan.

None of these drinks is that fancy. In fact, some of them are downright cheap. But when they're drunk in the right setting, they miraculously all just work. And that, of course, is no accident – because they've all, in their own way, evolved to suit the culture and palate and climate. And what can be bought in the corner shop.

So I'm including a chapter on highballs – though they may seem too lowly for words. Because they're what most of us actually drink most of the time – they're the folk songs of the cocktail world.

If in doubt, with a highball, use more ice. Make sure your mixers are very cold. And don't even think about garnishing with that slice of lemon that's now more than two weeks old.

I think a G&T is at its best when it's not too tinkered-with. But changing the garnish is an easy way to give it a bit of a twist. A big wedge of pink grapefruit looks beautiful. Cool, clean flavours like fennel, cucumber and celery can be nice, too. A sprig of rosemary, thyme, basil or lemon verbena, or a spritz of cocktail essence (**see** *The Garnish – p.67*) would add flavour and scent. For a G&T with a bit more edge, try adding a dash of bitters or a splash of Campari.

REBUJITO

The Andalusian answer to the isotonic drink is enjoyed across southern Spain, but is particularly associated with the Feria de Abril, the week-long fair that takes place in Seville each spring. Tangy, light and incredibly refreshing. 7-Up never tasted so good.

GLASS: *highball*

GARNISH: *lemon and lime wheels, mint*

METHOD: *build over ice*

75ml fino or manzanilla sherry

100ml 7-Up, Sprite or other lemon & lime soda

CUBA LIBRE

A classic rum and coke, but with just a little bit more to it. Orange bitters would be another way to give this drink a twist.

GLASS: *highball*

GARNISH: *lime wedge*

METHOD: *build over ice*

50ml light rum

10ml lime juice

2 dashes Angostura Bitters

125ml Coca-Cola

PALOMA

It's the combination of citrus and salt that makes this Mexican highball so exceptionally thirst-quenching. Traditionally it's made with Squirt, a grapefruit soda pop. But I like it best with at least some real grapefruit juice – try the Pink Grapefruit Mixer from Two Keys.

GLASS: *highball*

GARNISH: *grapefruit slice*

METHOD: *build over ice*

50ml tequila

10ml lime juice

120ml grapefruit soda

Pinch of salt

AMERICANO

It's easy to underestimate the Americano because it's so simple to make. But this sparkly, bittersweet, ruby-red aperitivo is one of the all-time greats.

GLASS: *rocks or highball*

GARNISH: *half an orange wheel*

METHOD: *build over ice*

50ml Campari

50ml red vermouth

50–75ml soda water

WHISKY HIGHBALL

The bars of Tokyo opened my eyes to how good (and how glamorous) a whisky soda can be. I watched bartenders serve my grandfather's dusty old drink with five-star ceremony. Hand-cut ice may be out of the question, but a nice glass and a good garnish is a start. Twists of orange, lemon, grapefruit (or even a mix) for sweeter whiskies; mint and/or lemon for peatier ones. Dry, refreshing and sophisticated.

GLASS: *highball*

GARNISH: *grapefruit and/or orange twist or mint and/or lemon*

METHOD: *build over ice*

50ml single malt or blended whisky

100ml soda water

PORTO TONICO

If you're looking for a lighter alternative to the G&T, this Portuguese sundowner is just the ticket. Bottled at around 20% abv – or half the strength of gin – white port has an aromatic, dry taste a bit like vermouth. Taylor's Chip Dry is crisp and herbaceous – very good with tonic.

GLASS: *highball*

GARNISH: *orange or lemon slice and a sprig of mint*

METHOD: *build over ice*

50ml white port

100ml tonic

PUNCHES & CUPS

Some of my happiest memories have been forged over a bowl of punch. It's the style of drink I most like to make for parties and large gatherings.

A big bowl of punch says: welcome! It says: come and be refreshed. And because you can knock it up all in one go, it's also a lot less faff.

The classic punch is built on five pillars: strong (spirit), sweet (sugar or liqueur), sour (citrus), weak (water or tea) and spice (bitters or nutmeg). There are various rhymes people use to remember this – but their formulae rarely pan out. I find it easier to think of the punch as a tarted-up, watered-down sour. Then it's simple to pull around.

The cup was a Victorian invention – the most famous example is Pimm's. There are many riffs on the theme but wine often figures, along with liqueurs and gin. A cup should be refreshing and fragrant, crowned with flowers and fruit: mint, borage, slices of lemon, orange and strawberries. Bring the whole garden in.

All these recipes can be made by the bowlful. They can also be served from a jug. Quite a few can also be bottled and chilled down the night before. They don't mind what glass they are served in. Or what garnish you put on top.

What really unites them, though, is the communal spirit in which they are meant to be drunk. They are convivial, generous recipes – a gift for the guest and host alike.

NOTES ON MAKING PUNCHES & CUPS

All the recipes in this chapter make roughly 1.8 litres
(around 2.8 litres once the ice is added), or approximately
12 x 150ml servings.

Once you've mixed your punch or cup, leave it to rest on ice for
five minutes or so before serving, so the drink can cool down
and the flavours have time to marry and infuse. If the drink
is destined to spend a long time on ice, serve it over one big,
slow-melting ice block.

Lastly, remember that punch-making is an inexact science
– and that should be embraced. In the 18th and 19th centuries,
when British punch culture was at its height, the construction
and refinement of a recipe could provide whole evenings of
entertainment, with everyone getting stuck in. So expect to
make adjustments – and always have a little extra of all your
ingredients on hand just in case it needs a tweak.

For more tips on making party drinks, **see** *Cocktails for a
Crowd – p.74.*

PINEAPPLE RUM PUNCH
TWO WAYS

This punch is the mixological equivalent of a choose-your-own-adventure book. Just the little tweak at the end – bitters or absinthe – takes it in two entirely different directions. Absinthe is a snappy partner for pineapple (I would happily use even more). If you're unsure of the tastes of your guests, though, Angostura Bitters might be a safer bet.

GARNISH: *pineapple rum chunks, lime wheels and mint*

METHOD: *mix and serve in a bowl or jug, over ice*

700ml pineapple rum*
120ml lemon juice
120ml lime juice
190ml sugar syrup
650ml soda water
and **5–7.5ml** Angostura Bitters
or **20ml** absinthe

*To make pineapple rum: peel and core a ripe pineapple and chop it into bite-sized chunks. Put the chunks in a large Kilner jar, cover with a 70cl bottle of rum (dark/golden is best), and steep for 12 to 24 hours (much longer, and it starts to go over the top). Strain off the pineapple chunks and set aside for the garnish. Use the rum immediately, ideally, but definitely within 24 hours.

GIN CUP

Once you've tasted this gin cup, you will never go back to Pimm's – it's a little more work, but the taste is far superior. This kind of cup is often mixed with fizzy lemonade, which I find a bit sweet – I prefer it with tonic, which gives it a drier bite. Pile high with garnishes but especially cucumber (or borage), citrus and mint.

GARNISH: *sliced citrus, mint, borage, cucumber, strawberries – the more the merrier*

METHOD: *combine in a big jug or bowl, over ice*

300ml gin

300ml red vermouth

300ml triple sec

900ml tonic (or sparkling lemonade)

SOUTHERN BELLE PUNCH

The combination of tannic Earl Grey tea, bitters and bourbon give this tawny punch a bit more edge than your average tropical fruit-fest. The longer it sits on ice, it seems, the better it gets. The absence of any fizzy ingredients means you can prep and bottle it the night before. Adapted from a recipe in *Batched & Bottled* by Max and Noel Venning.

GARNISH: *ice block and lemon wheels*

METHOD: *combine in a bowl over a big block of ice*

400ml bourbon

150ml lemon juice

150ml sugar syrup

40ml Luxardo Maraschino Liqueur

5ml Angostura Bitters

400ml cold Earl Grey tea

650ml chilled water

BADMINTON CUP

Charles Dickens was an enthusiastic compounder of punches and cups, and this Sangria-like recipe is said to have been one of his favourites. It's so easy to put together and looks lovely, too – it's one I often use for big gatherings. Don't open special wine for this; cheap and fruity is best. And don't feel you have to stick to lemon juice either – it's also good with a mix of freshly squeezed lemon, lime, pink grapefruit and/or orange juices (even better, in fact).

GARNISH: *cucumber (or borage, if you've got it), lemon and orange wheels and a light grating of nutmeg*

METHOD: *serve in a 3-litre bowl over a big block of ice*

600ml cheap red wine

150ml sugar syrup

150ml triple sec

300ml lemon juice (or a mix of citrus juices)

600ml soda water

PUNCHES & CUPS /

157

TEQUILA & LEMON VERBENA PUNCH

I make this punch every summer when lemon verbena's sherbetty scent is at its height. The recipe is by Nick Strangeway, one of the most talented flavour-smiths I know.

GARNISH: *lemon verbena sprigs and sherbet peels — you cannot use too much*

METHOD: *combine, peels and all, over a big block of ice*

300ml tequila

150ml lemon juice

150ml lime juice

100g orange and lemon sherbet (with peels) (**see** *Sugar Syrups – p.34*)

100ml lemon verbena syrup (**see** *Sugar Syrups – p.32*)

1 litre soda water

RIESLING CUP

This refined cup is based on a recipe from *The Savoy Cocktail Book* – the wine's zingy citrus and stone-fruit notes give it a wonderful tang. I used a dry German Riesling, but a sweeter style may require less liqueur. If you're not sure, mix it with half measures of each liqueur to begin with, and then taste and adjust as you see fit. The garnishes add colour and scent – do not leave them out!

GARNISH: *orange wheels, pieces of pineapple and mint*

METHOD: *serve in a 3-litre bowl over a big block of ice*

1.2 litres dry Riesling
120ml Grand Marnier
120ml Luxardo Maraschino Liqueur
600ml soda water

MULLED APPLE PUNCH

By the time Christmas comes round I'm heartily sick of mulled wine – I much prefer this hot punch with its apple and ginger kick. If you haven't got Calvados apple brandy, it's good with cognac, too. If you don't have ginger liqueur, you could substitute with ginger cordial. If your apple juice is on the sweeter side, you may need less honey, or even no honey at all. All that stirring, tweaking and tasting is very much in the spirit of punch.

GARNISH: *clove-studded orange slice and a grating of fresh nutmeg*

METHOD: *combine all ingredients in a saucepan and heat (but don't boil) for 10 minutes. Serve in mugs or sturdy punch glasses.*

230ml Calvados apple brandy (or cognac)
230ml ginger liqueur (or cordial)
1 litre cloudy apple juice
100ml lemon juice
20ml honey
320ml boiling water
1 clove-studded orange
6 star anise
1 cinnamon stick
A few orange and lemon wheels

A FEW MORE DRINKS EVERYONE SHOULD MAKE ONCE IN THEIR LIFE

Cocktail taxonomy is never simple – here are some one-offs, classics and oddities that for one reason or another I couldn't bear to leave out.

BLOODY MARY

The perfect Bloody Mary recipe is highly subjective. But I think it's much improved by the addition of sherry and celery salt – two ingredients that really amplify the umami. I'm also not averse to using a good-quality spiced tomato juice if one is available. Shaking a Bloody Mary, or serving it over ice, can turn it thin and watery – it's better to stir with ice and strain, or serve chilled, straight from the fridge. You could also rim the glass with a mix of salt, pepper and spicy shichimi for extra firepower.

GLASS: *rocks/ small juice glass*

GARNISH: *any combination of celery stick, lemon slice and spicy salt and pepper rim*

METHOD: *stir ingredients with ice to chill and then strain. Serve without ice.*

50ml vodka or gin

150ml tomato juice

15ml dry sherry

2 dashes Worcestershire sauce

3 dashes Tabasco

1 grind pepper

2 pinches celery salt

10ml lemon juice

COSMOPOLITAN

The Cosmo is not my favourite drink, I won't lie – but it's a part of the cocktail canon. The best formula I've found is this one by Simon Difford (which calls for plain vodka, but would also work with lemon vodka).

GLASS: *cocktail glass*

GARNISH: *orange twist*

METHOD: *shake and strain*

30ml vodka

30ml triple sec

45ml cranberry juice

15ml lime juice

1 dash orange bitters

ESPRESSO MARTINI

There are many ways to make an Espresso Martini. This is mine. It's really important to use very hot coffee, as this will give you the frothy head on the drink. Using lots of ice will chill it fast, without diluting it too much.

GLASS: *cocktail glass*

GARNISH: *three coffee beans*

METHOD: *mix the first four ingredients in the bottom of a shaker, add the piping hot coffee and shake with lots of ice. Strain.*

30ml vodka

30ml coffee liqueur

15ml golden/dark rum

5ml sugar syrup (optional)

30ml very hot, very strong espresso

HANKY PANKY

This spiky classic was created in the early 1900s by Ada Coleman, one of the very first women to tend the American Bar at The Savoy. Bitter, spicy, sweet, intense – wonderful stuff.

GLASS: *cocktail glass*

GARNISH: *orange twist*

METHOD: *stir and strain*

45ml gin

45ml red vermouth

2.5ml Fernet-Branca

LAST WORD

This jade-green classic is a bit of a secret handshake among bartenders and Chartreuse fans. It contains a lot of liqueur on paper, I know, but it's one seriously sophisticated sour. Also good blended with ice.

GLASS: *cocktail glass*

GARNISH: *nothing*

METHOD: *shake and strain*

25ml gin

25ml lime juice

25ml Green Chartreuse

25ml Luxardo Maraschino Liqueur

LONDON CALLING

When the Soho speakeasy Milk & Honey opened in 2002, it changed London's cocktail landscape – but like many of the city's great haunts, lockdown did for it in the end. The night before it closed, I went along for one last drink – and this is what I had. One of their bestsellers.

GLASS: *cocktail glass*

GARNISH: *orange twist*

METHOD: *shake and strain*

50ml gin

15ml fino sherry

10ml lemon juice

7.25ml sugar syrup

2 dashes orange bitters

MOJITO

The Mojito is often destroyed by over-muddling – I much prefer to shake it, as it gives you a fresher, brighter drink.

GLASS: *highball*

GARNISH: *mint sprig*

METHOD: *shake everything but the soda water and strain into a glass full to the brim with cracked ice*

50ml white rum

25ml lime juice

12.5ml sugar syrup

8 mint leaves

50ml soda water to top

MAI TAI

This Tiki classic has been much corrupted but done the right way it's sensational – its name comes from the Tahitian for 'out of this world'. This is my slightly simplified take on the recipe originally created by Trader Vic in 1944.

GLASS: *rocks*

GARNISH: *mint sprig, plus citrus slices, cherries, whatever you can throw at it. But definitely mint.*

METHOD: *shake and strain over cracked ice*

50ml aged rum

15ml orange curaçao (or triple sec)

20ml lime juice

10ml orgeat

5ml sugar syrup

NEGUS

The toddy-like Negus was a popular drink in Victorian times, especially during Twelfth Night celebrations. It's usually made with sherry or port, but it would work with pretty much any fortified wine. The little grating of nutmeg adds warm, sweet spice.

GLASS: *mug or robust glass*

GARNISH: *grated (shredded) nutmeg*

METHOD: *mix the first four ingredients well in the mug/glass, add hot water and stir*

75ml port or sherry

25ml lemon juice

½ tsp finely grated (shredded) lemon peel

5ml sugar syrup or honey

50ml boiling water

PEGU CLUB

The Pegu Club was a British officer's club in what is now Yangon, Myanmar – this was their house cocktail. A stiffener of the old sort.

GLASS: *cocktail glass*

GARNISH: *lime twist*

METHOD: *shake and strain*

50ml gin

20ml Grand Marnier or other orange curaçao

20ml lime juice

1 dash Angostura Bitters

5ml sugar syrup (optional)

RAMOS GIN FIZZ

This cloud-like confection from New Orleans is a bit of a palaver to make – but the result is exquisite: scented, silky and zesty. Hard shaking is key to achieving the required airiness. In its heyday it was prepared by a line of 20 'shaker boys', who'd all take turns agitating each drink.

GLASS: *small highball or flute (no ice)*

GARNISH: *orange twist and a small mint sprig*

METHOD: *shake everything except the soda water with ice, really really hard. Strain the cocktail off the ice into one half of the shaker. Hold that half of the shaker in one hand and the soda in the other and carefully pour two-thirds of the cocktail and a little of the soda into the glass so the two streams converge and the drink fluffs up. Let the head settle for a few seconds and then top up with the rest of the cocktail.*

50ml gin
15ml lemon juice
15ml lime juice
20ml sugar syrup
25ml egg white
25ml single (light) cream
3 drops orange flower water
Soda water

SGROPPINO

I've seen Italians practically come to blows over the correct recipe for a Sgroppino – some like it with cream, others consider that heresy, some like a dash of lemon juice, some don't. It was a sorbet maker in Turin who advised me to garnish with ground coffee. The name means 'to untie', as it's traditionally served as a refreshing digestif at the end of a meal or between courses.

GLASS: *cocktail glass*

GARNISH: *lemon twist and a pinch of freshly ground coffee*

METHOD: *time is of the essence here. In a small jug, quickly whip the sorbet, lemon juice and vodka, add the sparkling wine (and cream), stir briefly and pour into the glass. A little splash of sparkling wine just before you serve it will make it froth up beautifully.*

1 generous scoop lemon sorbet

15ml lemon juice

20ml vodka

40ml sparkling wine

10ml single (light) cream (optional)

SHAKY PETE'S GINGER BREW

I judged the cocktail competition that bartender Pete Jeary created this drink for – and have since watched its fame spread all over the world. Essentially a turbo-charged shandy, it's best prepared by the jugful and enjoyed on a hot day.

GLASS: *rocks*

GARNISH: *none*

METHOD: *blitz the gin, lemon and syrup with a couple of ice cubes for a few seconds. Pour into the glass and top with ale.*

25ml gin

30ml lemon juice

30ml ginger syrup (**see** *Sugar Syrups* – p.33)

60ml British bitter ale such as London Pride

SHERRY COBBLER

The Sherry Cobbler was born in the 19th century around the same time that sales of commercial ice took off – it's named after the 'cobbles' of ice over which it's served. A joyful riot of tangy, fruity flavour. Also good with ruby port instead of sherry, and maraschino instead of triple sec. Straw essential.

GLASS: *highball*

GARNISH: *the more the merrier – lemon and orange slices, a pineapple wedge, berries, a sprig of mint. And a straw.*

METHOD: *muddle the fruit in the bottom of the shaker. Add the other ingredients and shake with ice. Strain over cracked ice, churn and keep adding ice until the glass is full to the brim.*

A big handful of chopped-up citrus fruit, skins on, and peeled pineapple chunks

100ml sherry

25ml maraschino

10ml sugar syrup

1 dash fruity golden rum (optional)

WHITE RUSSIAN

Low-down, dirty and utterly delicious.

GLASS: *rocks*

METHOD: *build over ice*

50ml vodka

25ml coffee liqueur

50ml whole milk or full-fat oat milk

INDEXES

ALPHABETICAL
BY COCKTAIL NAME

A

Air Mail 144

Amaretto Sour 142

Americano 150

Apple & Bay Leaf Sour 145

Artichoke Spritz 133

Aviation 84

B

Badminton Cup 157

Basil & Honey Daiquiri 102

Basil Smash 85

Bloody Mary 160

Boulevardier 108

Bramble 86

C

Champagne Margarita 122

Coffee Negroni 111

Corpse Reviver No. 2 87

Cosmopolitan 162

Cuba Libre 148

D

The Daiquiri 100

Daiquiri Elixir 102

E

Espresso Martini 162

F

Fig Leaf Old Fashioned 97

Flamingo Gimlet 136

French 75 84

Frozen Orange Negroni 111

Frozen Watermelon Daiquiri 104

G

Gibson on the Rocks 90

The Gimlet 134

Gin Cup 156

The Gin Sour 82

Grapefruit Gimlet 136

H

Hanky Panky 163

Hemingway Daiquiri 103

Hibiscus Margarita 123

The Highball 146

Hugo Spritz 130

J

Jasmine Tea Martini 92

L

Last Word 163

Lime & Basil Spritz 130

London Calling 164

M

Mai Tai 165

The Manhattan 114

Manhattan 1890s-style 119

Maple & Bacon Old Fashioned 96

The Margarita 120

Martinez 91

The Martini 88

Mexican Jumping Bean 125

Mint Julep 98

Mojito 164

Monte Carlo 99

Mulled Apple Punch 159

N

The Negroni 106

Negroni Sbagliato 109

Negus 166

New York Sour 143

Nordic Martini 93

O

The Old Fashioned 94

P

Paloma 149

Passionfruit Daiquiri 105

Pegu Club 166

Penicillin 142

Pineapple & Cardamom Daiquiri 105

Pineapple & Shichimi Margarita 124

Pineapple Rum Punch 154

Pink Grapefruit & Chilli Margarita 125

Porto Tonico 151

R

Ramos Gin Fizz 167

Rebujito 148

Reverse Manhattan 116

Riesling Cup 159

Rob Roy 119

Rome with a View 131

Rosé Spritz 133

Rosehip Gimlet 138

Rum Old Fashioned 99

Rusty Manhattan 118

S

Sazerac 96

Sencha Tea Collins 87

Sgroppino 168

Shaky Pete's Ginger Brew 168

Sherry Cobbler 169

Sidecar 145

Silver Bullet 139

Smoky Martini 93

Southern Belle Punch 156

The Spritz 128

T

Tarragon Gimlet 137

Tequila & Lemon Verbena Punch 158

Tomato Gimlet 139

Tommy's Margarita 122

V

Vesper Martini 90

Vieux Carré 116

W

Watermelon Negroni 108

Whisky Highball 151

The Whisky Sour 140

White Manhattan 117

White Negroni 110

White Russian 169

Y

Yuzu & Jasmine Spritz 132

BY FLAVOUR

agave syrup **35**
  Mexican Jumping
    Bean **125**
  Pineapple & Shichimi
    Margarita **124**
  Tommy's Margarita **122**
almond: Mai Tai **165**
  orgeat **23**
apple: Mulled Apple
    Punch **159**
  Apple & Bay Leaf
    Sour **145**
artichoke: cynar **25**
  Artichoke Spritz **133**

basil: Basil & Honey
    Daiquiri **102**
  Lime & Basil Spritz **130**
bay leaf: bay leaf syrup **33**
  Apple & Bay Leaf
    Sour **145**
blackberry: Bramble **86**
  crème de mûre **24**

cherry: Aviation **84**
  Hemingway
    Daiquiri **103**
  Last Word **163**
  Luxardo Maraschino
    Liqueur **20, 35**
  Martinez **91**
  Riesling Cup **159**
  Southern Belle
    Punch **156**
coffee **26**
  coffee liqueur **22**
  Coffee Negroni **111**
  Espresso Martini **162**
  Mexican Jumping
    Bean **125**
  White Russian **169**
cranberry juice
  Cosmopolitan **162**

ginger: ginger liqueur **25**
  ginger syrup **33**

Mulled Apple
    Punch **159**
  Penicillin **142**
  Shaky Pete's Ginger
    Brew **168**
grapefruit: grapefruit
    juice **28**
  Grapefruit Gimlet **136**
  grapefruit syrup **33**
  Hemingway
    Daiquiri **103**
  Pink Grapefruit &
    Chilli Margarita **125**

hibiscus: Hibiscus
    Margarita **123**
honey: honey syrup **35**
  Air Mail **144**
  Basil & Honey
    Daiquiri **102**
  Penicillin **142**

lemon **28**
  Amaretto Sour **142**
  Apple & Bay Leaf
    Sour **145**
  Aviation **84**
  Badminton Cup **157**
  Basil Smash **85**
  Bloody Mary **160**
  Bramble **86**
  Corpse Reviver No.2 **87**
  French 75 **84**
  The Gin Sour **82**
  London Calling **164**
  Mulled Apple
    Punch **159**
  Negus **166**
  New York Sour **143**
  Penicillin **142**
  Pineapple Rum
    Punch **154**
  Ramos Gin Fizz **167**
  Sencha Tea Collins **87**
  Sgroppino **168**
  Shaky Pete's Ginger
    Brew **168**

Sidecar **145**
Silver Bullet **139**
Southern Belle
    Punch **156**
Tequila & Lemon
    Verbena Punch **158**
The Whisky Sour **140**
lemon verbena: lemon
    verbena syrup **32**
  Tequila & Lemon
    Verbena Punch **158**
lime **28**
  Air Mail **144**
  Basil & Honey
    Daiquiri **102**
  Champagne
    Margarita **122**
  Cosmopolitan **162**
  Cuba Libre **148**
  The Daiquiri **100**
  Daiquiri Elixir **102**
  Flamingo Gimlet **136**
  Frozen Watermelon
    Daiquiri **104**
  The Gimlet **134**
  Grapefruit Gimlet **136**
  Hemingway
    Daiquiri **103**
  Hibiscus Margarita **123**
  Last Word **163**
lime juice **28**
  Lime & Basil Spritz **130**
  Mai Tai **165**
  The Margarita **120**
  Mojito **164**
  Paloma **149**
  Passionfruit
    Daiquiri **105**
  Pegu Club **166**
  Pineapple &
    Cardamom
      Daiquiri **105**
  Pineapple & Shichimi
    Margarita **124**
  Pink Grapefruit &
    Chilli Margarita **125**
  Ramos Gin Fizz **167**
  Rome with a View **131**
  Rosehip Gimlet **138**
  Tarragon Gimlet **137**
  Tequila & Lemon
    Verbena Punch **158**

Tomato Gimlet **139**
  Tommy's Margarita **122**
maple syrup **35**
  Maple & Bacon Old
    Fashioned **96**
mint: Hugo Spritz **130**
  Mojito **164**

orange: Badminton
    Cup **157**
  Corpse Reviver No.2 **87**
  Cosmopolitan **162**
  Frozen Watermelon
    Daiquiri **104**
  Gin Cup **156**
  orange curaçao **22**
  Mai Tai **165**
  Pegu Club **166**
  Riesling Cup **159**
  The Margarita **120**
  triple sec **19, 35**
  Sidecar **145**

passionfruit: Passionfruit
    Daiquiri **105**
pineapple: Pineapple &
    Cardamom Daiquiri **105**
  Pineapple & Shichimi
    Margarita **124**

rosehip: rosehip syrup **33**
  Rosehip Gimlet **138**

tarragon: tarragon syrup **32**
  Tarragon Gimlet **137**
tea **29**
  Sencha Tea Collins **87**
  Southern Belle
    Punch **156**
  Yuzu & Jasmine
    Spritz **131**
tomato: Bloody Mary **160**
  Tomato Gimlet **139**

watermelon: Frozen
    Watermelon Daiquiri **104**
  Watermelon
    Negroni **108**

yuzu: yuzushu **24**
  Yuzu & Jasmine
    Spritz **132**

ALTERNATIVE INDEX

CHAMPAGNE (STYLE) COCKTAILS

Air Mail **144**

Champagne Margarita **122**

French 75 **84**

Negroni Sbagliato **109**

COCKTAILS FOR BOTTLING

Boulevardier **108**

Hanky Panky **163**

The Manhattan **114**

The Martini **88**

The Negroni **106**

The Old Fashioned **94**

Sazerac **96**

COCKTAILS FOR HISTORY BUFFS

Corpse Reviver No. 2 **87**

Hanky Panky **163**

The Manhattan **114**

The Manhattan 1890s-style **119**

Martinez **91**

Sazerac **96**

COOLING COCKTAILS FOR HOT DAYS

Frozen Orange Negroni **111**

Frozen Watermelon Daiquiri **104**

Hibiscus Margarita **123**

Rosé Spritz **133**

Sgroppino **168**

Shaky Pete's Ginger Brew **168**

GUILTY PLEASURES

Amaretto Sour **142**

Espresso Martini **162**

Frozen Watermelon Daiquiri **104**

White Russian **169**

HERBAL COCKTAILS

Basil & Honey Daiquiri **102**

Basil Smash **85**

Mint Julep **98**

Mojito **164**

Tarragon Gimlet **137**

Tequila & Lemon Verbena Punch **158**

LIGHTER-STYLE COCKTAILS

Americano **150**

Rebujito **148**

Yuzu & Jasmine Spritz **132**

MODERN CLASSICS

Bramble **86**

Cosmopolitan **162**

Espresso Martini **162**

Shaky Pete's Ginger Brew **168**

SAVOURY/SMOKY COCKTAILS

Bloody Mary **160**

Penicillin **142**

Rob Roy **119**

Smoky Martini **93**

Tomato Gimlet **139**

SECRET HANDSHAKES

Corpse Reviver No. 2 **87**

Hanky Panky **163**

Last Word **163**

Silver Bullet **139**

SPICY COCKTAILS

Bloody Mary **160**

The Margarita **120**

Mulled Apple Punch **159**

Pineapple & Shichimi Margarita **124**

Pink Grapefruit & Chilli Margarita **125**

Shaky Pete's Ginger Brew **168**

6-BOTTLE BAR

Gin Sour

Basil Smash

Sencha Tea Collins

Martini

Jasmine Tea Martini

Gibson on the Rocks

Negroni

Gin & It

Watermelon Negroni

Boulevardier

Frozen Orange Negroni

Old Fashioned

Fig Leaf Old Fashioned

Mint Julep

Bacon & Maple Old
    Fashioned

Gimlet

Tomato Gimlet

Grapefruit Gimlet

Tarragon Gimlet

Rosehip Gimlet

Sweet/Perfect/Dry
    Manhattan

Reverse Manhattan

Whiskey Sour

Americano

Gin & Tonic

12-BOTTLE BAR

Gin Sour

Aviation

French 75

Basil Smash

Sencha Tea Collins

Martini

Jasmine Tea Martini

Gibson on the Rocks

Martinez

Negroni

Gin & It

Negroni Sbagliato

Watermelon Negroni

Boulevardier

Frozen Orange Negroni

Daiquiri

Hemingway Daiquiri

Basil & Honey Daiquiri

Frozen Watermelon
    & Mint Daiquiri

Pineapple & Cardamom
    Daiquiri

Passionfruit Daiquiri

Spritz al Bitter

Hugo Spritz

Rome with a View

Old Fashioned

Rum Old Fashioned

Fig Leaf Old Fashioned

Bacon & Maple Old
    Fashioned

Mint Julep

Gimlet

Tomato Gimlet

Grapefruit Gimlet

Tarragon Gimlet

Rosehip Gimlet

Sweet/Perfect/Dry
    Manhattan

Reverse Manhattan

Whiskey Sour

Sidecar

Air Mail

Gin Cup

Southern Belle Punch

Pineapple Rum Punch

Tequila & Lemon

Verbena Punch

Mai Tai*

Mojito

Ramos Gin Fizz

Pegu Club*

Americano

Paloma

Gin & Tonic

Cuba Libre

*STRICTLY-SPEAKING, THESE
TWO CALL FOR ORANGE
CURAÇAO, BUT YOU COULD
FUDGE IT WITH TRIPLE SEC.

ACKNOWLEDGEMENTS

The Cocktail Edit started life during lockdown as a series of Friday night Instagram posts. So I should start by raising a glass to everyone who stopped by my virtual bar during that strange time to share cocktail recipes, shoot the breeze or simply say *cheers*. You spurred me on to write this book – and reminded me of the transformative power of the cocktail hour.

Thank you to Sarah Lavelle, Celine Hughes and everyone at Quadrille Publishing for taking the idea for *The Cocktail Edit* and running with it – it has been a real privilege to work with you. And so much *fun*.

Thank you Maeve Bargman for the stunning design and for remaining so good-natured in the face of my endless revisions; and to Laura Edwards, Joss Herd, Polly Webb Wilson and Jo Cowan for creating the cocktail pictures of my dreams.

Salud to Emily Lapworth, Nick Funnell and the eagle-eyed Sofie Shearman. If there's a drop too much absinthe anywhere in this book, you've only got me to blame.

Thank you to all the bartenders and flavour-smiths who gave me permission to feature their recipes, or adapted versions of them: Monica Berg, Mark Diacono, Simon Difford, Richard Godwin, Michael McIlroy, Joerg Meyer, Jeffrey Morgenthaler, Nick Strangeway, Max & Noel Venning, the team at the late, great Milk & Honey and everyone at Cantina Ok!.

Big love to Georgia Preston, Chloe Gott and Robert Caskie – thank you for keeping my show on the road. And to the friends and colleagues who – whether they knew it or not – helped shape the ideas and ambitions for this book: especially Victoria Moore, Diana Henry and Sam Walton and Heather Roche.

And thanks last, but not least, to my family: to darling Al for being my co-pilot, pacer and extremely studious taster; Mum and Dad for always being the source of such good cheer. Alfred and George – you may not be old enough for cocktails yet, but you've opened my eyes to what can be achieved with soda water and a curly straw. When you're ready to write the book, let me know.

AUTHOR BIO

Alice Lascelles is a journalist, drinks writer and
presenter. She writes a popular column for the
Financial Times covering wine, spirits and cocktail
culture and can often be found talking about
drinks on the TV and on BBC Radio 4. She's been
named Fortnum & Mason Drinks Writer of the
Year, Spirits Communicator of the Year at the
International Wine & Spirit Competition and is
also a Keeper of the Quaich.

She lives in London with her husband, two sons
and cocker spaniel Daisy.

@alicelascelles
www.alicelascelles.com